ENDOR

Lynn Davis is a woman of passion for Jesus. Not just for relationship with Jesus, but to reflect Him in her life, ministry and writing. Through this anointed book she is doing just that, and unlocking the door for others to follow, by highlighting a major key God is re-emphasizing in this hour. The key is speaking life over ourselves, our loved ones, and surrounding, often opposing, circumstances. As we get free and delivered from negative, un-Biblical mindsets and belief, and speak in line with God, and His Word, we will see change in circumstances, relationships, health and every area of life. As I preach, coach, minister online, and teach, I see the need for these principles in this hour. Most importantly, I commend this book because the principles feed my spirit, challenge my mindsets, and give me wisdom keys to see change in my own life. I am sure it will do the same for you.

—Ryan Miller, Pastor, Life Coach

It is my honor to share my feelings about Lynn R. Davis' book, *Deliver Me From Negative Self-Talk.*

As an emotional person, I tend to let life paralyze me with everything "negative" has to offer mind, heart, trust, self-esteem. When at a moment in my life I was looking for a form of consolation, an identifying source, I happened upon Ms. Davis' book.

When I began reading page after page of real experience, real talk, and scripture to back it up, the years of negativity, hurt, and anxiety began to release drop by drop as tears streamed down my face. My biggest battles are in this book, someone else has fought them too. God has given His anointed words of healing, through *Deliver Me from Negative Self-Talk,* to share with those of us who cannot write.

As Ms. Davis shares examples of real situations and real answers, the power of God washes over the reader and leads shattered hearts and minds to the road of healing.It is a book that was written, guided by the hands of God through the author. This book is a must-have for anyone who, like me, needs some real talk about negativity and how to rise above it.

—In my Master's service, Lynn Hankins, Singer/songwriter.

Deliver Me From Negative Self-Talk will give you the tools to defeat your biggest enemy, which is most times the inner "ME." If we are being completely honest, we fight mainly with ourselves to reach our full potential in life. As more people learn about this book, we're going to see a whole new group of successful, happy people living the life of their dreams! Great work Lynn!"

—Kelly Cole, Minister,
Bestselling author of *Solomon Wealth Formula*

One of the greatest obstacles to success and mental and emotional wholeness is negative thinking. As a therapist I am constantly talking to my clients' about negative thought patterns, cognitive restructuring, and learning to speak and think positive regardless of what is going on. Where the mind goes the body will follow. Lynn Davis has done a wonderful job of explaining to the reader biblical principles that govern the kingdom of God. If we as Christians don't learn to speak faith found in the Word of God, we can never be free from the demonic strongholds that the enemy has bound us in. This is a simple, yet profound book that puts the reader in the right direction to fulfilling their purpose and destiny. Any change happens in the mind before it ever manifests. Learning to think and say faith words is a process, but it is necessary. Deliverance is possible. The power is in the tongue. This book is a great resource that is a life-changer to all who read it.

—Samaria M. Colbert, Therapist and Author

DELIVER ME *from* NEGATIVE SELF-TALK

NEW & EXCLUSIVE
CONTENT

*A Guide to Speaking
Faith-Filled Words*

LYNN R. DAVIS

DESTINY IMAGE® PUBLISHERS, INC.

P.O. Box 310, Shippensburg, PA 17257-0310

"Promoting Inspired Lives."

This book and all other Destiny Image and Destiny Image Fiction books are available at Christian bookstores and distributors worldwide.

Cover design by: Cross and Crown

For more information on foreign distributors, call 717-532-3040.

Reach us on the Internet: www.destinyimage.com.

ISBN 13 TP: 978-0-7684-0767-9

ISBN 13 eBook: 978-0-7684-0768-6

For Worldwide Distribution, Printed in the U.S.A.

6 7 8 / 19 18 17 16

DEDICATION

This book is dedicated, with love, to my parents, Gene and Bertha Davis—to my mother, who dragged us six kids to church nearly every day of the week and taught me the power of faith and prayer. I love you mama and miss you. To my father, who taught me that love has no boundaries and that abundant living is about more than material gain.

"*God cannot give us peace and happiness apart from Himself, because it is not there. There is no such thing.*"
—C. S. Lewis

"*Relentless, repetitive self talk is what changes our self-image*"
—Denise Waitley

CONTENTS

INTRODUCTION

This is neither a deep theological study nor a breakthrough in the psychology of self-talk. It is, instead, a message of hope and inspiration from the Father to you. It is a guide inspired and completed with you in mind. To bless your life. To help you escape the bondage of fear and anxiety by renewing, not only your mind, but your mouth (words). God wants you happy. He wants you fulfilled and at peace. No matter what you are facing, peace is possible. Open your heart and let Him in. Allow Him to lead you to a new state of mind. One that over-flows with peace and joy. An emotional Garden of Eden where your life is beautiful, every need is met in abundance, and your soul prospers. The joy of the Lord is truly your strength. God is love, and He loves you so much. He wants you to know that you are fantastic in His eyes. You were created by love, for love, and in love. Nothing can ever separate you from it. You are a magnificent physical expression of God's unconditional love for all of mankind. When you accept that truth, nothing can stand in your way. God is faithful. He cares about how you feel. He cares what you experience, and He wants you to know that He's heard your prayer for help.

Speaking and believing grant us access to salvation. Romans 10:9 says, "That if thou shalt confess with thy mouth the Lord Jesus, and shalt believe in thine heart that God hath raised him from the dead, thou shalt be saved." This Scripture offers a very important principle—confessing with our mouths and believing in our hearts. Based on that premise, if we say it and believe it, we shall have it. That's both good news and bad. If you're speaking blessings, favor, and deliverance that is what you will have. But unfortunately, if you've been confessing *I'm tired, broke, and sick,* you're going to have just that.

You're going to reap the words that you sow. Whether you hear yourself talking or you're listening to someone else, words can and do plant seeds in your mind. Those seeds, if tended, will grow. What are you listening to on a regular basis? Are you listening to yourself condemn and criticize all day? Or is there someone near to you who fills your ears with gossip and defamation? If your ears are being filled with negativity, you're going to have to change that and quick. Take your ears somewhere else. If you can't remove yourself from the environment, learn to speak up and change the subject. If the problem is you, it's time to make some changes. Listening to negative words will only activate fear. If faith comes by hearing the Word of God—life—then it stands to reason that fear comes by hearing the opposite—words of death and despair.

When we hear the Word taught, preached, or recited, it is sown into the soil of our minds. As we think about the words we hear, something happens in our spirit. If we're open and receptive, we begin to feel uplifted and encouraged. We may even shout *Hallelujah!* or *Amen!* The more we meditate on the Word, the more we believe it. Before long we're not just thinking and believing, we're talking about it too. Faith comes from hearing God's Word (see Romans 10:17). Fear subsides, faith increases, and doubt has to surrender. Change what you hear, and you will change what you think. Change what you think, and you will change your life.

The Self-talk Cycle: Thinking, Believing, and Speaking

This cycle of thinking, believing, and speaking happens so quickly. It's almost like you have no control of it, but you really do. It's just going to take some effort—a bit of work on your part to really pay attention to what's going into your ears and how it is affecting your thoughts and beliefs. Once you learn to be more aware of what you are hearing, you will be able to identify what influences your self-talk. Once you identify the negative influence, you can use the wisdom of Scripture and biblical principles to turn negative patterns to positive.

In this book, you will learn to:

- Evict negative thoughts before they influence your thinking.

- Replace negative self-talk with faith-filled words.

- Clean out the clutter in your heart that is causing you to doubt.

- Respond to negative emotions before they get out of control.

- Believe, expect, and receive the unconditional love of God that will deliver you from chronic negative self-talk once and for all.

Even if you feel like you're going through hell and there is no way out, this book can help. I promise you, there is always a way out with God. Whatever problem you face, He has already provided the solution. Deliverance is possible, but you must receive it by faith.

I know you don't want to be negative. You want joy. You want peace. And you're ready to make the necessary shift in your thinking to make it happen. That encouraging nudge in your spirit is confirmation—change is possible. Not only is it possible, it's necessary, for the impact you will have on others and the Kingdom of God is great. Your peace will open the door for someone else's peace. Your deliverance will encourage someone else's. This journey begins with you.

So how do you reverse the negative cycle of toxic thinking? How do you eradicate negative self-talk? The process starts with three key areas—your heart, your mind, and your mouth. Until you master the condition of your heart, what occupies your mind, and what comes out of your mouth, you will continue to spiral.

What You Will Find in This Book

The message of *Deliver Me from Negative Self-Talk* is grounded in Scripture and biblical principles. I share personal and real-life experiences, some very intimate and sorrowful, that are relatable and engaging. The goal is to teach you how to use the Word of God to overcome the toxic thoughts and self-destructive communications that are holding you back from your joy and wellness and personal achievement.

Your Bible will be your number-one tool. I encourage you to use it in conjunction with this book. Study each Scripture reference to gain greater insight. Make it your mission to understand and be led by the Spirit—our Teacher, Comforter, and Guide.

At the end of each chapter you will find Faith Declarations, Discussion Questions, and Positive Speaking Guides along with personal accounts and biblical examples for inspiration. The last section of the book includes 30 Daily Meditations to help reinforce, motivate, and uplift you on your journey to a more positive life.

Faith Declarations

Your faith is the key. It's not just your attitude or the words alone, it's your belief in the words. You must have complete confidence that what you declare is more than just a possibility. It is reality. Not because of your individual power, but because of the Father's power flowing in you. In Exodus 4:12, God told Moses to "go, and I will be with thy mouth, and teach thee what thou shalt say." Then in Jeremiah 1:9, God touched Jeremiah's lips and said, "I have put my words in thy mouth." In both cases the emphasis is on the power of His words. Words can hurt, and they can heal. They can bind you or they can free you. Remember:

Faith comes by hearing. We *need* to hear ourselves speaking faith-filled words.

The Faith Declarations at the ends of the chapters are meant to encourage you. They are inspired by Scripture. Some may resonate so strongly in your spirit that you shed a tear. When that happens, and it will, copy those declarations and paste them around your home or workspace. Meditate on them and receive the promise by faith. Read the words and recite them with confidence; knowing that as you do, you are speaking God's perfect will for your life.

Discussion Questions

Discussion questions can be found at the end of each chapter. They will, hopefully, expand your thinking and encourage you to dig deeper. If you're reading with friends, that's all the better. The chapter questions can serve as starting points for your group conversations.

Questions sometimes facilitate a greater level of personal engagement. They may spark a thought, change your perception, or even become a personal call to action. Use them as a tool. I talk later about analyzing thoughts and thinking on a higher level. One of the best ways to develop critical thinking skills is to ask questions. The more you ask, the clearer you will be about what to focus on in order to become the positive, God-inspired believer you were created to be..

Faith-Filled Speaking Guides

Matthew 15:11 says, "It's not what goes into your mouth that defiles you; you are defiled by the words that come out of your mouth" (NLT). What comes out of our mouths is a reflection of our thoughts and the condition of our hearts. How we communicate is an indication of our level of spiritual maturity. As you're reading this book and working faithfully toward renewing your mind, you may realize that you need a little guidance when it comes to positive, faith-filled words you should say, as opposed to the negative words you were used to.

The guides at the ends of the chapters are there to offer some aid by providing examples of Scripture-based phrases that you may use to replace negative thoughts and comments.

Short Daily Scripture Meditations

You can begin your day with the devotions or read them before going to bed, in which case the Word of God will be the last thing on your mind before you fall asleep. Do what works for you. I vary from day to day. There is no right or wrong. This is your journey. Each day, you will read one devotion, giving you the opportunity to meditate on the promises of God for an entire month.

Devotionals lift your spirit and remind you that God is ever present. It's so easy to get down on yourself with all the standards that society has set for so-called success. Your success in overcoming negative self-talk is not just tied to renewing your thinking, but also to embracing God's unconditional love, grace, and mercy. Love empowers you to demand better for yourself. You have the grace to overcome every obstacle on your journey to a more positive you.

Shortly after releasing the self-published version of *Deliver Me from Negative Self-Talk*, I received several comments.

Most were positive. But one caught me off guard. The reader described the book as "a little fake-it-till-you-make-it book." I was disappointed. It was never my intention to lead readers to believe all they had to do was name it and claim it. There is so much more to our faith than that.

The world's perception, if I may put it bluntly, is life sucks and then you die. Keep in mind, not everyone will receive the revelation of Proverbs 18:21. You may get a few frowns and eye-rolls when you talk about being more positive. That's okay. You're not in this to please others. Just work on you. God will do the rest. As long as you know the truth—that you can change your life for the better—you can think and talk your way into a blessed life. You can be healed and delivered. Life is a journey with ups and downs, but it doesn't have to be miserable. Living a miserable existence is a choice. The misery begins in the mind and overflows into our reality. We can change that. Living an abundant life is possible. Calling those "things that be not" as though they were is possible for those who believe.

There's nothing fake about the Word of God. Don't be discouraged by pessimists. Resist opinions that you are trying to "fake it until you make it." There's nothing fake about confidence in God's Word or His promises. Your spirit is perfectly healed and whole and the power of God dwells in you. It is knowing that power intimately that will deliver you from negative self-talk.

Whatever area of your life needs healing, it can be healed and made whole again—your body, finances, relationships, emotions. Think God-thoughts. Speak life. Circumstances will change.

Chapter 1

WHY NEGATIVE SELF-TALK IS A HUGE PROBLEM

'Tis a strange mystery, the power of words!
Life is in them, and death...
Anger and fear are in them; grief and joy
Are on their sound; yet slight, impalpable.
—LETITIA ELIZABETH LANDON
(August 14, 1802–October 15, 1838)

In the Bible, we see Satan deliberately attack Job, killing his children, destroying his property, and infesting his body with boils. What happened to Job was not his fault. Sometimes things happen through no fault of our own. There is a very real enemy who wants to sift us as wheat (see Luke 22:31). But other times, we have ourselves to blame. With our lips, we curse ourselves and others. We speak gossip, lament, and complain. Every word is doom, gloom, and death. We think only of the worse-case scenario. We believe only what we see. Our tongue becomes our judge, jury, and executioner.

Proverbs 18:21 says, "Death and life are in the power of the tongue." The words we speak will either give life or cause death. They are powerful. Just as God created the heavens and the earth by speaking words, we too can create the life we desire by thinking and speaking faith-filled words. The same power that created the world resides in us.

Everything is made of something that cannot be seen by the naked eye. Billions of tiny atoms form molecules and make up matter. Sound waves travel through matter at high speeds. The words we speak create energy and vibrate throughout the universe. In the beginning, God spoke His energy and the universe came into existence. Think about that for a minute. Your attitude, words, and actions are energy. When released into your atmosphere, they cause change—good or bad—affecting the balance of every setting. Words affect everything. A yelling parent can set a child on edge and making them nervous or even ill. Studies have shown that words affect plant growth. Plants actually thrive when you talk to them. There's no denying words change environments.

That brings us to the problem with negative self-talk. What you are saying the most is affecting your environment the greatest. If your words are predominantly negative and pessimistic, so is your environment.

What Is Self-talk and Where Did It Come From?

Self-talk is the chatter in your head. It's what we say to ourselves about ourselves and others. Our inner voice chatters on and on all day until, if we're lucky, we fall asleep. Whether we want it to or not, it speaks.. At times it acts as a personal advisor, telling us what to say, what to wear, and how to act. It talks nonstop about anything and everything that you allow. This constant internal communication is our *self-talk*.

Earlier I mentioned the cycle of thoughts, beliefs, and speech. Self-talk begins with a thought. Once you start to believe the thought, it becomes part of your core beliefs, and a cycle begins. Repetitive negative thoughts contribute to your belief system. All of those strongly held assumptions manifest in the form of more negative thoughts. The more you think a thought, the more you invite more thoughts just like it. Is it any wonder your communication becomes toxic? But it doesn't have to be. Self-talk can be positive.

Not All Self-talk Is Bad

Most of our self-talk is useful and relatively harmless. No one gets offended and nobody gets hurt. Like when I scold myself for not making a list and forgetting to buy toilet paper. I huff, puff, get into the car, and go back to the store. But there have been other instances when my inner chatter hasn't been so harmless, like the day I blew a job interview. I knew it the moment the interview ended. The voices in my head tormented me on the ride home: "You're so stupid." "You're never going to get a good job." "They're probably trashing your application right now."

Those types of voices are mean. They are aggressive and, they may even make you cry. If you frequently think thoughts like, "I give up," "I can't do it, I can't go on without them," and, "I'll be dead in six months," you have an issue with negative self-talk.

At any given time, we can be attacked physically, emotionally, or spiritually. Satan is on the prowl, looking for someone to destroy, and he shows no mercy. That's why we are told in First Peter 5:8, "Be alert and of sober mind. Your enemy the devil prowls around like a roaring lion looking for someone to devour" (NIV). When we're going through tough times, we are especially vulnerable to negative thoughts. It's easy to focus on what is happening and take our eyes off of the Word. When you have an alert and sober mind you are aware of what's happening around you. Sober-minded people understand that hurtful thoughts are not of God, and they work to replace healing thoughts with poisonous thoughts.

How the Enemy Uses Negative Self-talk against You

Satan wants to keep you locked away in a prison of negativity so that you become powerless—ineffective in your home, in your career, and in the lives of the people you touch. The enemy knows if he can get you to spend your days focused on what's wrong, then it's "game over." He has won. In that state of mind you will be too consumed with doubt to train your children in the way they should go, be a supportive spouse, minister to the hurting, or pray for the sick. When you're bogged down in the mires of negative self-talk, you don't spread the Gospel. Instead, you spread gossip and carnality. Negative self-talk is like a contagious disease that mutates and spreads, infecting yourself and all with whom you come in contact.

You may be thinking, *"But my negative self-talk isn't that bad."* Second Corinthians 2:11 warns us not to be ignorant of the enemy's devices. He has many ways of deceiving the believer. One of those ways is by making it seem as if our thoughts and words have no power. Whatever you are saying or thinking is creating what you are experiencing. If there is something in your life right now that you do not want, the enemy has very subtly taken what you've been thinking and saying and used it against you. No matter how insignificant your thoughts or words seem, if they aren't helping you, they're hurting you. Make a conscious effort to be aware of what you're thinking and saying. Are you giving the enemy an opportunity to use your mind and mouth to harm yourself and others? Ephesians 4:27 says, "Do not give the devil a foothold" (NIV). Paul was encouraging the Church to express their anger in a way that was not destructive or divisive. He wanted them to be aware that the enemy would use their enmity against them and others. Don't give him ammunition to use against you. When a negative thought comes to mind, refuse to give the enemy a foothold.

Choose to Speak Life

Think for a moment about the situation in your life that is causing you the most grief. Are your thoughts predominately negative? When you discuss it, what are you saying? In your heart of hearts, how do you feel about it?

You must know the answers to those questions if you are to address the issue of self-talk. If your mouth, mind, and heart are all negative, there is no doubt in my mind that your situation is negative as well.

It's time to try something different. Instead of talking about how terrible your relationship is, confess that the relationship is godly and all is well. If you want something positive to happen in your life, stop dwelling on the negative. Instead of complaining and doubting, give faith-filled words a chance. Speak life to your circumstance.

Rather than talking about how terrible your life has become or how miserable your situation is, why not say what you want? Why not confess that your partner has a godly attitude and all is well? Why not choose to say what God says? This doesn't mean that you can name it and claim it. No. There is more to deliverance, breakthrough, and manifestation than "claiming it." You are experiencing what you believe to be true. If you're failing, it's because you've been believing you are a failure. When you change what you believe and say, you will change what you experience.

Believe that God wants you to live a blessed and victorious life at whatever level you are. Believe that God still can and will do miracles. Believe that God loves you enough to care about what you are going through. Believe that He will move on your behalf if you just believe in Him. Believe that your choice to think God-thoughts and practice speaking what God says will change your life. It changed mine. I promise it will change yours too.

For most of my life, I lived as a self-proclaimed pessimist. I expected the worst, and I got it. My attitude was, if you expect to be disappointed then it won't hurt as bad when it happens. I think about that now, and I cringe. My relationships, finances, and life in general were disappointing. I wasn't happy, and I didn't think I was supposed to be. I thought only perfect Christians deserved God's love and prosperity. In my mind, I was a mediocre Christian, at best. It's no wonder I was miserable—I was inviting misery into my life with my thoughts, my speech, and my attitude.

One day, after crying my eyes out yet again, I prayed for answers. I'd been beat up by life. I was tired of being disappointed, mistreated, and stabbed in the back. There had to be more to this existence than church, work, home, and waiting to die so that I could be happy in Heaven. So many of my brothers and sisters are living this same "less than" life. God never intended that. Heaven is a wonderful experience to look forward to, but there is so much more God wants us to enjoy right now. A better life is possible. The minute you choose thoughts and words of life, you have unlocked the door to endless possibilities of joy, peace, and Heaven on earth.

Think about good things like the ones listed in Philippians 4:8, which we'll talk more about later. Choose thoughts that uplift you. Words that reflect the living Word of God. Study Scripture, declare it, and believe it. Let His Word become your words. Jeremiah 1:9 reads: "Then the Lord reached out His hand and touched my mouth and said to me, 'I have put My words in your mouth'" (NIV).

The Holy Spirit will fill us with wisdom and understanding of God's Word. He wants to lead us in our thoughts and speech. Speak as God speaks. Think as God thinks. Practice it all daily and watch what happens. We have the power within our own minds to live more abundantly. There is power in words—written, spoken, and conscious positive thinking.

"In the beginning was the Word, and the Word was with God, and the Word was God" (John 1:1 NIV). The Word is with us. When we make a choice to speak life, we have the power of the Creator supporting us. God has your back. When you deliberately speak life over your children, they will return home. Your finances must improve. Dead circumstances can be resurrected. It matters what you meditate on. What's on your mind will come out of your mouth, so you must, on purpose, put good thoughts in your mind. Place faith-filled words in your mouth, and believe with your whole heart that His Word will never return void. It will accomplish everything God intended for your life (see Isaiah 55:11).

DISCUSSION QUESTIONS

1. On a scale of one to five, with five being the most positive and one being extremely negative, how would you rate your self-talk?

2. What are examples of some of the negative and positive things that you say to yourself?

3. How do your words affect your environment and the people around you?

4. What did you learn from chapter one about the origins of self-talk?

5. What is your favorite takeaway from this chapter? How will you apply it to your spiritual walk?

Chapter 2

WHAT'S ON YOUR MIND?

Albert Camus said, "An intellectual is someone whose mind watches itself." Thinking is your mind talking. Your thoughts—they become words. Words become actions, and your actions create your character. The goal is to achieve a godly character, to become more like God in words and actions.

The personal commentator seated inside your brain gives you a blow-by-blow of your life's events. It critiques every detail of your life, offering advice, mostly unsolicited, about virtually everything—from how much you weigh to how little you've accomplished. At times it's also positive, angelic, and loving.

When the commentator is supportive and nurturing, it says things like: "You're a great person," or "Hang in there; you can do it!" These types of uplifting, motivational thoughts are examples of what's called *positive self-talk*. When the conversation is darker and the inner critic blames, criticizes, or discourages, the mental communication is then known as negative self-talk. For example, you'll have thoughts like, "You're not good enough," "You'll never be promoted," or "You're a failure."

By the way, you are not a failure. You are fantastic. You have greatness inside you. Perhaps you haven't tapped into it yet. Or you've allowed the negative committee in your brain to convince you that you can't be, won't be, or shouldn't be great. That's all a bunch of hogwash. The negative voices are garbage—all lies. Those hurtful, cruel, and evil voices are the ones we want to get rid of once and for all. God wants you to know that you are not a mistake. Your past does not define you. Neither does the "junk chatter" in your head. Don't let it convince you otherwise.

> *Do not conform to the pattern of this world, but be transformed by the renewing of your mind. Then you will be able to test and approve what God's will is—His good, pleasing and perfect will* (Romans 12:2 NIV).

Stop focusing on what you haven't done, or what you meant to accomplish, but haven't yet. The focus now is on accepting that you are loved by God, and there is nothing you cannot do with Him on your side. It's time to turn the tide on negative self-talk.

> *Set your minds on things above, not on earthly things* (Colossians 3:2 NIV).

Negative thoughts are spiritually impure and must be filtered through the Word of God. Any thought that makes you feel defeated, hurt, or insufficient is a *lie* and must immediately be spiritually purified. Only the Word can filter a negative thought pattern. Just because you thought it doesn't make it true. Does it match what God said in Scripture? That's the real test. If it doesn't, cast it down. Replace it with a thought based on a verse like Romans 8:39, "Nor height, nor depth, nor any other creature, shall be able to separate us from the love of God, which is in Christ Jesus our Lord."

Seek understanding. Pray for wisdom. Study for knowledge and you will receive it. For every problem you face, there is a solution. Remember First Corinthians 10:13, which promises, "There hath no temptation taken you but such as is common to man: but God is faithful, who will not suffer you to be tempted above that ye are able; but will with the temptation also make a way to escape, that ye may be able to bear it."

Find out what the Bible says about your situation. Hold that word in your mind and heart. Whenever the enemy shoots you a negative thought, cast it down and replace it with the life-giving Word.

Protect Your Mind

To the pure, all things are pure, but to those who are corrupted and do not believe, nothing is pure. In fact, both their minds and consciences are corrupted (Titus 1:15 NIV).

When my aunt was diagnosed with breast cancer, she'd tell me how people were constantly telling her negative stories about cancer patients who either died or suffered terribly.

Hearing these horrific stories only introduced more negative thoughts to the ones she already battled. Thankfully, after some quiet time of prayer and meditation she would replace those thoughts and the anxieties would subside.

When you're believing for healing in an area of your life, physical or otherwise, you can't afford to listen to other people's negativity. The enemy will gain a foothold; and before you know it, your thoughts will run wild with images of suffering and defeat, or worse—death. Guard your mind from any negative information that will distract you, regardless of who that information comes from—professionals, family, friends, the Internet, whomever. It will only discourage you and introduce doubt. Doubt is the arch enemy of faith, and continually entertaining negativity of any kind will only feed the doubt monster.

Stop negative people in their tracks. When they come to you with stories of bankruptcy, death, and despair, stop them midsentence and say, "I'm in faith for my deliverance, and I only want to hear success stories and good testimonies. Do you know any of those? I'd love to hear some."

When people are speaking negatively into your life, don't feel like you have to spare their feelings. You don't have to be rude or hurtful. But with love, let them know that what they are saying doesn't line up with what you are believing God wants to accomplish in your life.

If they don't understand where you are coming from, you may very well have to love them from a distance. It's possible that they don't have a revelation of the truth that you have. They don't understand the importance or the power of speaking life. "In their case the god of this world has blinded the minds of the unbelievers, to keep them from seeing the light of the Gospel of the glory of Christ, who is the image of God" (2 Corinthians 4:4 ESV).

Renewing Your Thoughts

Your thought patterns are not set in stone. Your mind can be transformed and renewed, and your renewed mind will take you into a place of healing and provision—a place that your old carnal, negative-thinking mind cannot even imagine. "Then He opened their minds to understand the Scriptures" (Luke 24:45 ESV).

The Word is life to those who find it and health to their flesh. Believe in the Word, not the world. "I have told you these things, so that in Me you may have peace. In this world you will have trouble. But take heart! I have overcome the world" (John 16:33 NIV).

Again, any thought that says otherwise is not coming from God. That's why we are instructed: "[Cast] down imaginations, and every high thing that exalteth itself against the knowledge of God, and bringing into captivity every thought to the obedience of Christ" (2 Corinthians 10:5).

When you're sick, your thoughts have a tendency to rebel against the Word of God. That's why you have to take control of them. Cast down negative thought patterns, regardless of what researchers, doctors, neighbors, or friends say. If their words aren't in line with what God says, then they're not words you should live by.

Don't be afraid to talk to yourself while you're thinking negative thoughts. Say, "No. That thought is a lie. The Word of God says. 'The Word is a lamp unto my feet, and a light unto my path'" (Psalm 119:105).

Healing Is Still Available Today

Jesus came that we might have life more abundantly. Whatever illness has invaded your body must be obedient to Jesus Christ, and leave. The Bible says that there is a way that seems right to men, but the end is destruction. There is a path that leads to healing. That path is Jesus. He is the Way the Truth and the Light. It may seem right to expect death from sickness and disease, but that is not the will of God. Know that God has another plan for your life.

That plan is an abundant life.

God is not caught off guard by your illness. He knew it was going to happen before you were born. He knew, on the day His Son was nailed to the cross, that it was going to happen. Don't dare give up on your healing because the doubt committee in your mind is telling you it's hopeless. Resurrection power resides in you. Think it. Speak it. Believe it; but most of all, *know* it. It is done in Jesus's name.

Speak words of life. You are the reason Jesus suffered and died at Calvary. Death is powerless over you. You are eternal. There is an appointed time for your healing. Though it may not look like it, though it may not happen immediately, "it will surely come" (Habakkuk 2:3)!

You can't speak sickness and death and expect healing. You can't think and speak poverty and expect provision to flow from heaven. God didn't create the world by meditating and talking about the darkness. He said, "Let there be light" (Genesis 1:3). Nurture your environment with positivity through the energy of your words. Speak abundance. Don't rehearse the worst-case scenario or what the doctor said *might* happen. If you feel pain or see a lump, lesion, or sore, reject the negative thoughts of disease.

Medical professionals have God-given skills and talent, but they don't have the last word. Christ had the last word. Even the apostles had a doctor with them in their travels. Luke, who wrote the third and longest gospel in the New Testament, was a physician. It's a blessing to have positive, committed, and experienced healing professionals in your midst.

Thinking on a Higher Level

Aim for a higher level of thinking. Don't allow negative thoughts to influence what you say or do. You're better than that. You're stronger. Take undisciplined irrational thoughts captive. Train your mind to transcend low-level negativity. Strive to think on a godly level. "And set your minds and keep them set on what is above (the higher things), not on the things that are on the earth" (Colossians 3:2 AMP).

High-level thoughts go beyond the negative and take you to a place of positivity—a heavenly place where the glory of God resides. There, you will find peace, victory, healing, and deliverance.

Philippians 4:8 says, "Finally, brothers and sisters, whatever is true, whatever is noble, whatever is right, whatever is pure, whatever is lovely, whatever is admirable—if anything is excellent or praiseworthy—think about such things" (NIV). All of these things are what I believe contribute to higher-level thinking.

Here are a few questions you can ask yourself that will help you analyze and spiritually discern your thoughts:

- Is the thought a Philippians 4:8 thought (good, lovely, admirable, etc.)? If it is not from God, just say no to it. You have to protect your mind.

- Does the thought make you feel blessed or burdened?

- Does the thought influence you to speak life or death?

- What can you find in Scripture that relates to the thought you are having?

By answering the questions above, you will help yourself to quickly differentiate negative thoughts from godly ones. You will reach the point where casting down negative thought patterns will become automatic. When an unhealthy thought comes, immediately you can say to yourself, "This thought is not God's best for me. I know that I can think much higher thoughts than this."

The Power of a Focused Mind

In First Corinthians 2:16, it says that we have the mind of Christ. We are liberated—heart, mind, and soul—through Jesus Christ. As we build a relationship with Him, we understand better how God thinks. The Holy Spirit guides us and teaches us the ways of the Lord, so that we act and think more like Him daily.

In Philippians 2:4, Paul discourages selfishness and pride. Those characteristics only lead to destruction. There is nothing to be gained from treating others as if they are lower than you. Christ very well could have snubbed the people around Him. As the Messiah, He could have walked around with His nose in the air, treating others as servants—but He didn't. Instead, He adopted an attitude of humility. In Philippians 2:5, Paul says, "Let this mind be in you, which was also in Christ Jesus."

Not to say that we allow people to take advantage of us. It's not about becoming a punching bag or doormat; it's about being an example for the world to follow. It's about having a mind that is stayed on Jesus. A mind that is fertile and produces positive thoughts. The very mind that will change our life for the better. Adopting the mind of Christ will motivate us to live lives of humility, peace, charity, and compassion. There is great strength in these attributes. When we sow these seeds into our future, we will reap the same—peace, love, and compassion—in our own lives in a greater measure.

When our minds are opened to the things of God, we will have purer thoughts. Those thoughts manifest in positive words and actions.

It's Dangerous to Speak Your Negative Mind

Murmuring, complaining, and unbelief caused the Israelites to wander in the wilderness for forty years! (See Numbers 14:30-35.) What are you saying that's causing your life to wander aimlessly in the wilderness of less than God's best? The Israelites were focused on the problems, not the promises. They complained about what they were going to eat, how long the journey seemed, who the leader was. When we're in the wilderness of life, it's easy to focus on feeling lost and afraid, but focusing on those feelings and verbally expressing them will only invite more of the same. Fear breeds more fear. Gossip breads more gossip. Negativity breeds more negativity.

Speaking your negative mind will only keep you in the place where you are. If you continue murmuring and complaining long enough, it will take you somewhere you don't want to go. You don't have to spend forty years in the wilderness.

Paul said, "When I was a child, I talked like a child, I thought like a child, I reasoned like a child. When I became a man, I put the ways of childhood behind me" (1 Corinthians 13:11 NIV).

Have you ever listened to a child speak? They are notorious for speaking their minds. You never know what they're going to say. If you're lucky it's nothing that will embarrass you or hurt someone else. Kids are kids. They have to be taught. They aren't mature enough to understand that their words are hurtful—both to others and themselves. The spiritually mature believer knows that what's on your mind isn't always the best thing to say. The Bible tells us that one day we will have to give account for every idle word that leaves our mouths (see Matthew 12:36).

The Mouth of a Mature Believer

God has promised long life to those who are able to control their tongue. "Those who control their tongue will have a long life; opening your mouth can ruin everything" (Proverbs 13:3 NLT). Self-control in this area is another sign of spiritual maturity. Immature people say whatever they feel, like children who have not been taught.

As we meditate on the Word and become more intimate with the Father, we understand more about communication and the appropriate manner in which we should speak. We grow and mature in the ways of God. Our mannerisms and behaviors reflect a greater level of maturity. The level that prays, "Let the words of my mouth, and the meditation of my heart, be acceptable in thy sight" (Psalm 19:14).

As kids we teased, "Sticks and stones may break my bones, but words will never hurt me." But the truth is words *can* hurt. With your words you choose life or death. We declare, "I am blessed," or "I am cursed." Mature believers choose blessings. "Out of the same mouth proceedeth blessing and cursing. My brethren, these things ought not so to be" (James 3:10).

No believer in his or her right mind would speak destruction over himself, his family, relationship, career, or health. What you complain about holds back the manifestation of God's promises. Matthew 15:11 says, "It's not what goes into your mouth that defiles you; you are defiled by the words that come out of your mouth" (NLT).

Sometimes we just need to seal our lips. "If you can't say something good, don't say anything at all." Our mouths can hold us back from promotions, end relationships, start fights, and get us into plenty of trouble.

Words can scar a child, wound a spouse, or kill a partnership. We read in Proverbs 29:11 the following warning: "A fool uttereth all his mind: but a wise man keepeth it in till afterwards." If the Bible says it's foolish to speak our minds, then why does society advocate it? Because that is how society operates. That's the world's way of handling problems. We have to remember that we are in this world but not of this world.

This power that we have to speak life is real. We have tremendous opportunity to call blessings and favor into every situation that we are involved in. We can heal relationships and people.

As believers we think before we speak. We think first with the mind of Christ, and then we speak words from the heart of God.

DISCUSSION QUESTIONS

1. What role does your mind play in negative self-talk?

2. What are some ways to renew your thinking?

3. On a scale of one to five, how well do you protect your mind?

4. What did you learn from chapter two about the importance of your focus?

5. What is your favorite takeaway from this chapter? How will you apply it to your spiritual walk?

Chapter 3

Do You Have a Heart Condition?

What does the condition of your heart have to do with your self-talk? Everything. Your beliefs and intentions are held in your heart. Unless you believe, the words that you are saying will be powerless. Your words alone have no power. It's God's power and anointing, mixed with your faith (belief), that brings breakthrough. Believe in your heart, without a doubt, that God can work through your words to move mountains, and those mountains will move. "Truly I tell you, if anyone says to this mountain, 'Go, throw yourself into the sea,' and does not doubt in their heart but believes that what they say will happen, it will be done for them" (Mark 11:23 NIV).

In the beginning it may be a challenge to believe something that is the opposite of what you are experiencing. That's okay. Keep believing by faith. It takes practice and consistency to undo the negative patterns you're used to. You are replacing old system of thought that got you to where you are. If you are sick, it's going to *feel* like a lie when you say,

"By His stripes I am healed." If you are in debt, it's going to *feel* strange saying, "Every need is met in abundance." Don't give in to your negative feelings. You can change your feelings. When you change what you think and say, you'll change what you believe and your feelings will adjust.

Rely on God's power, not your own. His power is mighty to the pulling down of strongholds (see 2 Corinthians 10:4). It's His power working in you that will transform your life. Clear away that blockage of doubt. Get out of self-mode and walk into God-mode. Put your faith in God. Doubting, fearing, and holding grudges clogs your heart. Every negative feeling that you allow to fester blocks the life-giving flow of faith from working in other areas of your life. No heart can function properly when there is blockage.

Heart Blockage

A heart filled with fear, doubt, unforgiveness, and the like has what I call blockage. The power of God cannot freely flow through it. Nor can it function on a higher level—God's level. But a clean heart opens the door for greater anointing, glory, and peace. The anointing flows unhindered, and in the midst of that flowing power of peace and glory you will find the freedom from negativity that you seek.

If you continually live in stress and turmoil, you put added unnecessary pressure on yourself and your ability to trust God for deliverance. Because you are in such a chaotic state, you will stay focused on everything that is going wrong, causing you to doubt the power of God. So even though you know, "Greater is He that is in me," (1 John 4:4) your blocked heart is saying, "I'm never going to get out of this mess." As a result, you stay in the mess.

Lay aside differences with others. Let go of the hurt you've been holding on to. Don't let the cares of this world hinder your progress. Pray for wisdom concerning the issues that weigh heavy on your heart. Nothing is worth forfeiting your victory. You can win this.

A young lady in a church I attended years ago treated me rudely whenever she saw me. She made it a point to look at me, roll her eyes, and then smile at some other person nearby. It was like she wanted me to feel bad. The first time I was really hurt. I'd never done anything to her. I didn't understand. The next time I saw her I greeted her. She didn't respond, but simply acted as if she didn't hear me. Part of me wanted to ask, "What's your problem?" But I knew that would only aggravate the situation. So I let it be. For the remainder of my time at that church, I chose to be civil. If I saw her, I smiled; I didn't worry about whether or not she would reciprocate. How she treated me was her problem, not mine. I needed my heart to remain open and clog-free. Besides, God's command to love is not predicated on another person's attitude toward us.

We can't get worked up over someone else's problem. Make no mistake. How someone feels about you is their problem not yours. Stay focused. You're working on your deliverance, prosperity, healing—you don't have time for petty things. Don't give the enemy a foothold. Think godly thoughts. Practice unconditional love and keep pressing toward the promise.

I wish that I could tell you that we became friends, but that's not the case. She remained cold and indifferent, but God did bless me with a peaceful spirit. My attitude changed. I didn't see her as a bad person. I saw her as a hurting person. The love of God in me manifested courtesy and politeness. "But watch yourselves lest your hearts be weighed down with dissipation and drunkenness and cares of this life, and that day come upon you suddenly like a trap" (Luke 21:34 ESV).

When my home was near foreclosure, I remember experiencing waves of anger, resentment, and fear. I couldn't see a solution, only the problem. The anger and fear threatened to block my faith. The lack of results in your life just may be because you are holding on to negative emotion that is blocking your breakthrough. No anger, fear, revenge, or otherwise is worth blocking your blessing.

Don't allow anything to stop the flow of the anointing in your life. Pray Psalm 51:10: "Create in me a clean heart, O God; and renew a right spirit within me." Let the Lord clear the blockage. Let Him free you of whatever is holding you back from receiving His best for your life. God wants to give you a clean heart.

Fill Your Heart with the Things of God

Scripture says, "A good man brings good things out of the good stored up in his heart, and an evil man brings evil things out of the evil stored up in his heart. For the mouth speaks what the heart is full of" (Luke 6:45 NIV). Your thoughts are going to take direction from what is in your heart and vice versa, and it won't be long before your mouth begins to articulate those thoughts.

Is your heart filled with love? Or is it filled with envy, strife, and confusion? David said in Psalm 119:11, "I have stored up Your word in my heart, that I might not sin against You" (ESV). If we're going to succeed, we must make sure our hearts are clutter-free and filled with faith.

Good Intentions Go a Long Way

God is interested in your intentions. Strive to please God with the intentions of your heart. Seek Him in all that you do. Live by faith. It is faith that pleases God. Trust and believe Him. Let your deeds and words reflect a healthy heart. Hebrews 4:12 says, "For the Word of God is living and active, sharper than any two-edged sword, piercing to the division of soul and of spirit, of joints and of marrow, and discerning the thoughts and intentions of the heart" (ESV).

Take inventory of your heart. Model the compassion and love of Christ always. In doing so, you will increase your faith and allow the glory of God to freely flow in your thoughts, emotions, and physical body. A heart that loves God and seeks His approval will be strong, healthy, and produce lasting fruit. Pray this prayer with me:

> *Father in Heaven, right now I ask that You would set a guard over my mouth. Let the words of my mouth and the meditation of my heart be acceptable in Your sight. Fill me with the compassion of Jesus for all those I come in contact with. I thank You, Lord,*

that I have the mind of Christ. My heart,
my mouth, and my mind belong to You. My
thoughts are Your thoughts. My words are
Your words. Out of the abundance of my
heart I speak life. In Jesus's name, amen.

The words we speak from a healthy heart will be words of life. The thoughts we think will be pure and godly.

God's words in your mouth are more powerful than you have imagined. Negative self-talk is the enemy. Don't accept it as normal. It is not. Make a habit of declaring what you desire, not what you despise. Your mind must be protected. Let the Word of God stand guard over your mind. Any impure thought should be treated as an uninvited guest. Let the Word of God seize it and evict it.

Declutter your heart today. Keep it free from clogs like anger, resentment, envy, and strife. Forgive and cast those cares on God. He cares about your pain. Believe the Word with all your heart.

Go easy on yourself. It will take some practice to get your heart, mind, and mouth all working together. God is patient with you. Be patient with yourself. Pay attention to whichever area requires more work. Give yourself a spiritual checkup. Ask yourself, "Is God pleased with the condition of my heart, my mouth, my thoughts?" Once you've answered, do the work. Tackle that area. Work on it until it falls in line with the Scripture, "Let the words of my mouth, and meditation of my heart, be acceptable in Thy sight" (Psalm 19:14).

Negative self-talk cannot control your life without your permission, but you do control it by faith. "Set a guard over my mouth, Lord; keep watch over the door of my lips" (Psalm 141:3 NIV).

You can be delivered from the demeaning, destructive self-talk that is ruining your relationships, health, spiritual growth—your life. Whether the battle is against illness, a disobedient child, or a wayward spouse, you can use the words of your mouth to take authority over the situation and change it. "Death and life are in the power of the tongue" (Proverbs 18:21).

FAITH DECLARATION

*My words are powerful. I use
them to uplift and inspire.*

I speak blessings, favor, and peace.

My tongue is writing a new story for my life.

*My mouth continually praises
and glorifies the Lord.*

*He is pleased with the words of my mouth
and the meditation of my heart.*

DISCUSSION QUESTIONS

1. What are examples of some of the negative and positive things that you carry in your heart?

2. What did you learn from chapter three about the condition of your heart?

3. What role does your heart play in negative self-talk?

4. What are some ways to declutter your heart?

5. Which area challenges you the most?

   - condition of your heart

   - your mouth

   - negative thoughts

6. What is your favorite takeaway from this chapter? How will you apply it to your spiritual walk?

Chapter 4

STOP TALKING ABOUT THE PAST

You build on failure. You use it as a stepping-stone. Close the door on the past. You don't try to forget the mistakes, but you don't dwell on it. You don't let it have any of your energy, or any of your time, or any of your space.

—JOHNNY CASH

Learn from the past but never live in it. The past is where it belongs—behind you. There is only room in your life for right now—today. This is the day the Lord has made. Rejoice and be glad in it (see Psalm 118:24). Forget about what happened to you then. Yes, then was painful. It left scars. When you think about it, you still shed a tear. But, dear loved one, God's love brought you out of that circumstance because it was not where He wanted you to be. Don't let your mind take you back where God delivered you from. Your physical body is free; now it's time to let your mind be free as well. When God makes you cry, it will be tears of joy, not sorrow. He is a God of miracles. Nothing compares to what God is going to do for you next.

Even though the Israelites witnessed the parting of the Red Sea, they soon forgot how God had delivered them from their enemy. God reminded them in Isaiah 43, but then He said something else, "But forget all that—it is nothing compared to what I am going to do" (Isaiah 43:18 NLT). Do you see? He said, *I delivered you from your past, but that's nothing compared to what I am going to do now and in the future.*

Whatever happened in your past, remind yourself that God delivered you then and that's nothing compared to what He's going to do next!

Past Pain: If You Hold On, You Might Pass It On

When negative memories of people or events from our past are allowed to linger, they affect our actions, our attitude, and our communication. We've heard time and again of the abused growing up to become the abuser. I know a young mother, in her late twenties, who experienced verbal abuse as a child. Her mother called her everything from a whore to a female dog. That young lady is now a mother herself, and she calls her own preschool-aged daughter those same names. So often women who were mistreated in their past carry baggage from that relationship into their future.

I know another woman, a bit older, who after her divorce swore off men completely for several years. Whenever the subject of men came up, she'd say things like, "All men are the same; good men are hard to find." She let the pain of her past haunt her future. It wasn't until she realized the resentment was hurting her that she stopped speaking negatively about men and subsequently found a wonderful, God-fearing husband.

A past colleague of mine grew up in the projects. She often reminisced about the days of eating mayonnaise sandwiches and sleeping on the floor because her parents couldn't afford furniture. As an adult she wasn't wealthy, but she had a nicely furnished apartment and a modest income. When she spoke of the past, a spirit of sadness seemed to come over her.

Though she had more, she still talked about not having enough and barely making ends meet. I told her what I'm telling you. Stop reliving the poverty of your past. Instead, try starting each day with prayer of thanksgiving. Here's an example of a thankful prayer: "Father, I thank You for all that You've blessed me with. By faith I know that I am abundantly supplied and every need in my life is met in Jesus's name."

I implore you, child of God. If it seems like your entire life you've been going round and round on the same negative Ferris wheel, it's possible it's because you're being dragged down by negative thoughts of your past. Let them go. Cut the ties. Don't speak of them anymore. Accept that it happened, but know that it doesn't define you. Forget the former things. God wants to do something better for you in your future, but He needs your cooperation.

To look at me you would never know that I was once a single mother on welfare. That I dropped out of college and once lived in a motel because I was homeless. My past isn't pretty, and the things I mentioned aren't even the half of it. But one thing I know that helped me move forward was not looking back. I prayed about the choices that I'd made and I learned to make better ones. I forgave the people who'd hurt me and let go of the ones who weren't heading in the same direction God was sending me. My life didn't miraculously improve overnight, but with time my heart healed. My life turned around. I went on to complete my bachelor's, obtain an advanced degree, and buy my own home. Every day I'm reminded that God is faithful. We all have a past, but it can only hold us back if we let it. Don't let your past hold you back.

The angels instructed Lot and his family to leave Sodom and not look back, but Lot's wife couldn't help herself. Even though there was nothing positive in Sodom for her to hold on to, she had to turn around and see what she'd left behind. Because she couldn't move forward without turning back, she was destroyed (see Genesis 19).

What you've left behind is not worth what is waiting for you ahead. Be grateful that you made it through, and get excited about where you're headed. Stop talking about your past. Declare your happy ending with your lips, and trust that God is faithful to accomplish His word.

God Cares about You, Not Your Past

You may be in a mess or coming out of a mess. Either way, God is concerned about you, not your past mistakes. He never left me in my mess, and He will not leave you. Even when you stray away from Him, He will pursue you like the Good Shepherd portrayed in Luke 15:

What man of you, if he has a hundred sheep and should lose one of them, does not leave the ninety-nine in the wilderness (desert) and go after the one that is lost until he finds it? And when he has found it, he lays it on his [own] shoulders, rejoicing (Luke 15:4-5 AMP).

Maybe you think you've made too many mistakes for God to forgive you. You couldn't be more wrong in your assumption. God is not like our friends and family. He doesn't hold things against us. When we repent and ask for forgiveness, He gives us a clean slate—a new beginning. We start anew as if our past never happened. It took me many years to understand and receive the gift of God's love and forgiveness. It was hard to grasp that He could love me, even though I had blatantly disobeyed His will. Besides, based on my experience, people "threw you away" when you did something they disliked. For years I believed God was the same. I believed that He didn't want anything to do with me because I'd messed up, and the only way to get back in God's good graces was to clean myself up and live a perfect life. But Isaiah 53:6 offers reassurance: "We all, like sheep, have gone astray, each of us has turned to our own way; and the Lord has laid on him the iniquity of us all" (NIV).

We don't have to clean ourselves up or try to perfect our imperfections. Jesus paid the price for all our sins, past and present. Stop repenting over and over again for the same sin that you committed last week or twenty years ago. God's forgiveness doesn't have an expiration date.

That past transgression that keeps nagging you, making you feel guilty or ashamed, is just being used by the enemy to hold you back. God has forgiven you and cast your sin into the sea of forgetfulness (see Micah 7:19). You are His child. You are the righteousness of God in Christ. Forgive yourself and move on. You will never accept the blessings that God has in store for you if you keep telling yourself that you don't deserve them. God wants you to live out your purpose. He wants you to experience a life of joy and peace and have a sound mind so others will see your good works and glorify the Father in heaven (see Matthew 5:16).

Your Past Does Not Cancel Out Your Purpose

When Rahab the harlot was approached by the Israelite spies for help, she could have turned them away. She could have said, "No, thanks. I'm not getting involved." But she didn't. She must have been scared, but she saw an opportunity to help God's chosen people. By faith she put her life and the life of her family in danger to support God's plan to deliver Jericho into the hands of the Israelites.

Considering Rahab's past as a prostitute, she could have talked herself into believing that she was unworthy to be a part of God's family. Instead, she displayed great faith, refusing to be held hostage by her pagan upbringing or her past sins.

Beloved of God, the same goes for you. Let it go. What you were in the past does not dictate what you are destined to become. The guilt you are feeling does not belong to you. It is a lie from the pit of hell. Send it back there. If you strayed,

God wants you back. Put your life in God's hands, and take your rightful place as a leader in the body of Christ where you belong. The faith hall of fame in Hebrews 11 is filled with examples of godly men and women whose faith pleased God and allowed them to overcome serious obstacles. He wants to add your name. He needs someone like you on His list.

You're not too messed up. You're not hopeless. No matter what you've done, don't let anyone plant seeds of condemnation into your future. They are not qualified to do so. My mother used to say, "People can say what they want, but they don't have a heaven or a hell to put you in."

Your past does not cancel out your purpose! God has the final say. It doesn't matter how messed up your life is or was, Jesus died for you and God loves you more than you can fathom.

I read an interesting social media post once that really stuck with me. It went something like this: "Noah was a drunk, David was a murderer and an adulterer, Peter was a coward, Judas was a backstabber, Jacob was a liar, Samson was a womanizer, Rahab was a prostitute, Elijah was suicidal, Moses had low self-esteem, and the Samaritan woman had multiple husbands...so what's your excuse?"

Remember, you have the power to live free from your sins through Jesus. Whatever you answered, it's covered by the blood of Jesus. Don't let what has happened in your past make you think you don't deserve to be happy or blessed.

When Jesus died on the cross, He already knew you were going to mess up. He already knew that you were going to be hurt. But He also knew you, being created in His image, had great potential. So you see, you are the reason He gave His life—so that your own life could be resurrected through Him. It's never too late. Trust God. Go to bed with a smile on your face. Get some rest and then get up and start again. God's mercies are new every single morning. Live the blessed life God planned for you from the beginning (see John 10:10).

You can re-create your life today by the power of your thoughts, actions, and words. God has given you this power by His Spirit, but you have to start somewhere. I always tell my oldest son, "It's never too late to head down the right path." As long as you're breathing, you have a chance to re-create yourself, your relationships, opportunities, and success with God's help.

Embrace the good news that you have that same power. It doesn't matter what capacity you are in—parent, son, daughter, business owner, or ministry worker, to name a few. Our tongues are ready writers, enabling us to speak the Word and create positive change.

When you spend years being hurt and disappointed by people who say "I love you," it's easy to project that same conditional "strings attached" type of love onto God. But we should never make that mistake. It holds us back from our destiny. God's love for us is unconditional. There are no strings attached. He loves you when you are great and when you are not so great, when you succeed and when you fail.

God Wants to Heal You

While putting on lotion one morning, I noticed the scar on my right calf. In the second grade, I burned myself leaning too close to a small gas heater while trying to get warm. The burn blistered in the shape of the letter *T.* I didn't realize that it had blistered until the pain started. By then I was already at school. My teacher noticed my discomfort and asked what happened. I showed her the burn and she immediately sent me to the nurse. The nurse gently applied medicated ointment to the area and wrapped it in gauze.

I don't remember how long it took to heal, but I do know that it wasn't overnight. Even though it's completely healed and painless today, there is still a scar. Maybe you have been badly burned by life and maybe you're still in pain. There is a balm in Gilead (see Jeremiah 8:22). Jesus is that healing balm. Life may burn us, but we can and will heal when we apply His love, grace, and mercy to whatever we are facing. God promises to heal, and His love will take away the pain.

Stop listening to the lies of the enemy. He is only trying to steal, kill, and destroy your faith. The Word instructs us to trust God and not our own understanding (see Proverbs 3:5). Furthermore, we are encouraged to acknowledge God in all things and know that He will direct our paths.

Know the truth. Stand boldly on it. God is for you; and while He is for you, nothing can be against you. Nothing can break you. Have faith first; ask questions later. There's victory in you, but you have to be hungry for it. You have to want it like you want air. We are made in the image of God. He is mindful of us because He values us. Keep yourself built up in your most holy faith. You're not washed up. You're coming up. Faith comes by hearing and hearing by the Word of God (see Romans 10:17). You're not down on your luck.

Dump the burden of baggage. A burden is anything weighing you down. Negative thoughts, fearful apprehensions, past mistakes, failures, screw-ups, and toxic relationships—they're all burdens, and that makes them baggage. There's no room for baggage on this trip. As Geoff Shaw said, "You only get to experience each minute of your life once."

"Lay aside every weight, and the sin which doth so easily beset us" (Hebrews 12:1). When negative thoughts creep in, don't dwell on them; replace them with thoughts of God's loving nature. How much He wants you to prosper in every area of your life. How He allowed His own Son to die for you, because you are worth dying for—isn't that just amazing? Say it with me: *I must be pretty special if Jesus, the Christ, thought I was worth dying for.* There is no greater love than a man who would lay down His life for a friend.

Your most important assets are on your person—your mind, heart, and spirit. You don't have to break down under the pressure. Meditate on God's Word day and night. Focus on what He says you can do, not what the world is telling you is impossible. For every negative news story you see on television, there is a positive scripture in the Word to encourage you. Your success depends on which of the two you spend your time focusing on. "I have set before you life and death… choose life" (Deuteronomy 30:19).

FAITH DECLARATION

I am redeemed. Christ has paid the price for my sins.

My past does not cancel out my purpose. I am not condemned.

My future is bright. I press toward a higher calling.

Nothing separates me from God's love.

I am spiritually mature. I am emotionally sound.

I am free to be the best I can be in Christ Jesus.

DISCUSSION QUESTIONS

1. Why is it counterproductive or harmful to dwell on the past?

2. How can past mistakes hold you captive?

3. What role does your past play in your purpose?

4. What negative patterns have you seen in yourself over the years that have held you back from living out your purpose?

5. How does your past life influence your current outlook?

6. Are you living out your God-ordained purpose? If so, how? If not, why? What negative aspects of your past could be holding you back?

7. How do you think God views your past mistakes? Do you believe that you are forgiven? Have you forgiven yourself?

Chapter 5

LEARN TO CONTROL YOUR NEGATIVE EMOTIONS

If your emotional abilities aren't in hand, if you don't have self-awareness, if you are not able to manage your distressing emotions, if you can't have empathy and have effective relationships, then no matter how smart you are, you are not going to get very far.
—DANIEL GOLEMAN

That part of your soul that can bring you great joy or cause you to experience much pain—your emotions. Your feelings, like your emotions, are just that—yours. They belong to you. You keep them under control. You're responsible for your actions—not the person who cuts you off in traffic, not the rude clerk at the mall, the unruly kid who tramples your garden, or the in-laws who behave more like out-laws. It's all you. It's all me. We have to own our behavior. It's not about what they do to us; it's about how we respond to what has been done.

When we respond with fury or rage, we are out of God's perfect will. If we know we have a tendency to get out of control, we need to acknowledge it and deal with it head-on. Even if there is some chemical imbalance or medical issue that is causing negative emotions to be out of control, that's no excuse; we still have a responsibility to deal with it. Negative emotions will fill your head with angry, vindictive, and sometimes violent thoughts that will only lead to you saying and/or doing horrible things to yourself and the people around you.

No medical condition gives us the right to walk around with an attitude as big as Texas. Nor does it give us a license to "speak our mind." We have a responsibility to walk in love at all times. Even on days when we feel not particularly loving or loveable.

If you've lost control of your emotions, chances are you're not happy. You don't have to live life in a crappy mood. You deserve to be happy. It's time to regain control. Take back your emotions and reclaim your peace and happiness. If you've never had any peace, let me tell you, it's better than gold. Gold is grand, but peace is priceless. By God's grace you're going to have it—all of the peace, love, joy, and emotional control you can stand.

You just have to love yourself enough to say, "Enough is enough!" You're not going to allow the negative voices in your head or the venomous comments of others to poison your thoughts and words and ultimately destroy your emotional health or your life. You're going to take back control of your life.

The good news is you can change things right now, today. It will take conscious effort and dedication, but you're not in this alone. God wants you to succeed. You are loved, right where you are. You don't have to start out emotionally well to receive God's love. You don't have to earn it or fix yourself first. You just have to stop sowing emotional turmoil. Stop giving the enemy a foothold in your emotions. The more you fly off the handle, the more people who push your buttons will be drawn to you.

God's grace is available to you right now in the middle of your messed-up emotional state. In First Peter 5:10 it says, "But the God of all grace, who hath called us unto His eternal glory by Christ Jesus, after that ye have suffered a while, make you perfect, stablish, strengthen, settle you." It may feel like your emotional pain will last forever, but God's grace is available to us in our times of temptation and travail. God wants to restore you, confirm you, strengthen you, and establish you. Isn't that awesome?

You don't have to be at the mercy of your circumstances. The world says it's natural to overreact. Sure, in the short term you feel vindicated by putting someone in their place, but if you truly are a man or woman of God you can never be at peace with acting out of your godly character. No amount of retaliation or vengeance will ever make you feel good about yourself. You're not wired that way. That's why, ultimately, you end up feeling sorry for your actions.

Uncontrolled negative emotions often lead to heated arguments or worse. We've all seen the horrible true stories on television of people whose emotions got the best of them.

Later, in the interviews, they wish they'd just walked away or made some other decision. Proverbs 15:1 says, "A soft answer turneth away wrath." You may think the opposite is true, but kindness through Christ-like behavior will always prevail. When you sow kindness, you will reap kindness. Maybe not from that particular person or event, but God will make it work in your favor.

Think of a time when you were in a bad situation. Maybe you're in one now. Did you have trouble controlling your emotions then? Are you having trouble right now controlling your emotions, even though you know you should?

God doesn't want you to suffer. He doesn't want you to hurt yourself or anyone else. He knows you are hurting. He knows you want to feel vindicated, but He doesn't want you to make the situation worse. He doesn't want to see you suffer more than you are in this moment. Your response to what's happening now will impact what happens in your life tomorrow. So He's encouraging you to take control. Step away. Take a deep breath. Count backward from ten. Whatever you need to do to keep it together. Try to detach yourself from the negative emotion and reattach yourself to His Word.

> Many are the [emotional] *afflictions of the righteous: but the Lord delivereth him out of them all* (Psalm 34:19).

Do something to take your mind off the situation. Read your Bible. Watch your favorite televangelist. Listen to music. Go for a walk to clear your head. If you need to cry, cry. If you just have to talk to someone, call a trusted mentor or person you really trust.

Speak with someone who will help you keep a level head. The last person you need to contact is an emotionally charged acquaintance who slashes tires and keys cars. You can come out on top even if you cry buckets of tears and feel like your heart is shattered. God heals, and His Son comforts us. "In the world ye shall have tribulation: but be of good cheer; I have overcome the world" (John 16:33).

Remember, the emotion you sow is the emotion you will reap. Don't let the enemy use stress to destroy you and the people you love. Control your emotions and manage your stress. Remember, "There hath no temptation taken you but such as is common to man: but God is faithful, Who will not suffer you to be tempted above that ye are able; but will with the temptation also make a way to escape, that ye may be able to bear it" (1 Corinthians 10:13). You can do it!

The Victory of Self-Control

You will experience a sense of victory over the situation when you are able to look at it without feeling vengeful or distressed. These emotions are not only unhealthy, they are unproductive and ungodly as they indicate that your faith is weak in that area. Positive Christians allow their behavior to reflect the love of God in the most difficult situations. There will be times when you will be angry. The Bible even speaks of anger: "Be ye angry, and sin not: let not the sun go down upon your wrath" (Ephesians 4:26). Accept that you are angry about the situation. You may even tell God, "Lord,

I'm angry." But don't stop there. Ask Him to give you peace and guidance as to how you should deal with the problem. Do not allow the anger to lead to vengeful or self-destructive behavior. David was in a terrible position for a time. He was hurt and angry, but he prayed to God. God came through for David—not right away as David had hoped, but in the end David reigned as king.

If you have the spiritual maturity and the emotional fortitude, you can search for the good in every situation. Even if you feel there is no good to be found, you can still decide to view the experience as a learning opportunity.

Seek the good and you will find the good. While on earth, Christ experienced hurt and pain from those who made themselves His enemies, but He still chose to love them. The entire time He walked with Judas, He knew that Judas would betray Him. But there is never any indication in Scripture that He treated Judas badly. When we seek to have the attitude of Christ toward others, we demonstrate Jesus's example of compassion for others. It's a choice to seek the good in others. A choice that is challenging and unpopular, but we aren't called to be popular. We are called to effect change.

Our behavior toward others should bring out the best in others. Matthew 5:13 asks the question, "But if the salt loses its flavor, how shall it be seasoned?" (NKJV). We are the salt of the earth, intended to improve the tastes of life. Our attitudes should never leave a bad taste in anyone's mouth no matter how much they hurt us.

David demonstrated how to love our enemy by seeking the good (see 2 Samuel 1:17-27). Even though Saul made

David's life miserable and even tried to kill him, David chose not to speak evil of Saul. Instead, David used his musical talent to write and perform a beautiful song for Saul's funeral. David chose to see the good in Saul. He choose to see Saul through the eyes of God. We are all His children, created by Him, and if God created your enemy surely there is something good in them. It may be buried under years of hurt and pain, but it's there waiting to be awakened or at least nudged by your Christ-like attitude toward them.

Chances are, something will happen this week that you won't like. The only way you will experience victory is by responding in faith. Instead of getting angry and upset, respond in love. Responding in love is our secret weapon. Why? Because love gets God's attention. God is love, and He loves you unconditionally. He wants you to know that you are fantastic in His eyes. You were created by love, for love, and in love. Nothing can ever separate you from it. You are a magnificent physical expression of God's unconditional love for all of mankind.

After all, God is love. Our love reaction pleases Him, so much that He comes to our aid. God won't respond to fear, but He will respond to faith. Responding lovingly in a negative situation is an act of faith. This week as you respond in faith, expect God to deliver victory on your behalf. Your response is key. Resist the tendency to react negatively. Stop, assess the situation, take a deep breath, and know that victory is possible with God. Walk in love, and watch God turn the situation around in your favor! You deserve to have a great week, and with God you can. Don't settle for anything less.

Keep the right attitude. Stay in faith. Go ahead; it's okay to be angry. You're bending when you're angry, but don't break. Don't lose faith, and do something that will derail your spiritual walk or cause more damage. Trust that God is faithful. Your deliverance is on the way, and you will reign over your circumstances!

Faith Declaration

I think godly thoughts.

The joy of the Lord is my strength.

I will focus on good things that make me smile.

*I seek the good in every situation,
and I dwell on the positive.*

*I spend more time seeking solutions
and meditating on answers.*

I have the mind of Christ, and peace is my gift.

DISCUSSION QUESTIONS

1. Why is emotional control so important?

2. What are some of the ways you can avoid losing control?

3. How do you personally manage stress? Are your methods effective?

4. What ways can you avoid losing control when dealing with someone else who has lost theirs?

5. If you were in a "turn-the-other-cheek" situation, would you be able to avoid losing control?

6. How does the enemy use stress against us?

7. What are some of the scriptures in this chapter that helped or encouraged you?

Chapter 6

DON'T BE DISTRACTED BY THE SHADOWS

The world that we live in is full of distractions and pleasures that pull us away from a spiritual life. Even our jobs, which are a very necessary and important part of our lives, can end up being the altar at which we pray.
—MICHAEL HUFFINGTON

Negative self-talk overtakes us when we become so distracted by problems that we take our eyes off the promise. Sometimes even those of us who have a strong relationship with Christ find ourselves losing focus and becoming distracted. Peter had a desire in his heart to walk on water—and he actually did—but somewhere between the first step and the second he began to doubt. He was thinking about what he, as a human, couldn't do.

When Peter began to sink, he cried out, and immediately Jesus reached out His hand and caught him. "You of little faith," He said, "why did you doubt?"

Notice Scripture says that Jesus reached out His hand and caught Peter. That implies to me that Peter must have been just an arm's length from Jesus. Though Peter was in reaching distance of Jesus, fear got the best of him and he began to sink.

I wonder if it was so dark that Peter couldn't see how close he was to Jesus. It would seem to me that if he could see that Jesus was just in front of him, the feelings of doubt wouldn't have been so strong. Sometimes we can be so close to experiencing our breakthrough; but because we can't see how close we are, we give in to the fear of not knowing, and we begin to doubt that we will ever make it.

Peter was right there close to Jesus, but he still doubted. He didn't doubt Jesus; he doubted himself. He was thinking about what he, as a human, couldn't do. When we take our focus off the power of God and begin to consider our own limited strength, we are headed for disaster. Peter was fearful of the roaring winds and crashing waves. He forgot that he was walking on water because of Jesus's power, not his own.

Scripture doesn't say Peter looked back at the boat. He was looking at the waves and observing the wind around him. When we take our focus off the power of God and begin to consider our own limited strength, we will get distracted. We will take our eyes off the Father. Look again at what happened to Peter. He stepped out of the boat, and after a few steps he began focusing on his surroundings. The wheels in his mind started turning, and his inner voice must have taken over. Can you imagine his negative self-talk? "You can't walk on water. You're going to drown. It's dark; you don't even know what's out there!"

How often do we do just what Peter did? How often do we take our eyes off the mighty power of Jesus within us and start focusing on other things around us and allow ourselves to be overcome with fear? *I can't make ends meet. I'm overweight. I'm a single mom. I'm not pretty enough. I didn't go to college. My marriage is failing. My kids are rebellious. My business is failing. What if I die?* Like Peter, when we're distracted we begin to sink.

Sinking is a state of mind. It's caused by focusing on all of the wrong things. Fix your eyes on the Lord. He knows the plans He has for you. Plans to make us prosper and not harm us. Plans to give us a hope and a future (see Jeremiah 29:11). If things are so bad that you're just too afraid to look, close the eyes of your soul and open the eyes of your spirit. We walk by faith, not by sight.

Don't let what's happening around you cause you to lose focus. It's all just a ploy of the enemy to distract you. Lift up your eyes and look to the hills where your help comes from. All of your help comes from the Lord (see Psalm 121:1-2). Declare it and believe it.

Friends and family can be distractions. They say things that do more harm than good. First, I want to say—anyone who truly loves you will never intentionally say words that will harm you. The people closest to us have the greatest ability to do the most harm. We love them, trust them, and listen to them. The enemy knows that and will use it to his advantage. Remember, it was Job's wife who told him to curse God and die.

Whether the negativity is coming from a lifelong friend, spouse, aunt, uncle, child, or favorite cousin—God is not directing this communication. The negative person is speaking from a place of fear, and "God hath not given us the spirit of fear" (2 Timothy 1:7). It's important that you understand and discern this.

I know you love this person, but if he or she is not encouraging you to hold fast to your healing, you're going to have to politely (in love) correct them. Your deliverance depends on it.

The Shadows Are Just Distractions

Yea, though I walk through the valley of the shadow of death, I will fear no evil: for Thou art with me; Thy rod and Thy staff they comfort me (Psalm 23:4).

Valley experiences are a part of life. I wish that I could tell you that every day will be perfect and stress-free, but I cannot. That would be a lie. The truth is: Believers face afflictions and challenges. We walk through valleys filled with shadows—but we don't go alone. Our heavenly Father is with us, leading us through however long the journey may take.

As you walk through the valley of difficult times, don't let the shadows scare you. They are just distractions. They cannot hurt you. Though they are large and threatening, they have no power. Jesus conquered death. It is powerless against Him. Its shadows are distractions to take your mind off the promises of God—promises of long life and eternal life.

Your valley experience is temporary. On the other side is victory. Shadows are meant to distract you from the reality.

The reality is that you are not going to stay in the valley, and nothing in the valley can hurt you as long as God is with you. He is your Shepherd, and He can guide you safely through any difficult situation.

Don't Be Distracted by Someone Else's Journey

And Jesus answered and said unto her, Martha, Martha, thou art careful and troubled about many things: but one thing is needful: and Mary hath chosen that good part, which shall not be taken away from her (Luke 10:41-42).

It's a waste of our time to be concerned about other people and how they are managing their spiritual walk. We each are responsible for our own salvation. God has not asked us to report to Him what someone else is doing—or not doing, for that matter. It can be very dangerous to become fixated on other people's journeys. In Luke 10:41-42, Martha was concerned about the wrong thing. She was so distracted by what Mary was doing, that she failed to see that she wasn't handling her own business.

When we allow ourselves to be distracted in this way, we risk losing focus in our own relationship with God. We leave ourselves vulnerable to the enemy's attacks, opening the door to jealousy, envy, and strife, which the Bible warns will open the door for every evil work (see James 3:16).

Close the door on the enemy. Don't give him an opportunity to come into your life and cause more problems than he already has. If you've been focused on someone else's life—stop. Pray that God will help you stay focused on your journey. Ask Him to show you what you can do to grow stronger. In First Thessalonians 4:11, we are instructed: "Make it your ambition and definitely endeavor to live quietly and peacefully, to mind your own affairs, and to work with your hands, as we charged you" (AMP).

When we mind our own affairs, we are less likely to become distracted and better able to focus on the things God wants us to do in our own lives and for the Kingdom.

Lay Aside Every Distraction

Wherefore seeing we also are compassed about with so great a cloud of witnesses, let us lay aside every weight, and the sin which doth so easily beset us, and let us run with patience the race that is set before us (Hebrews 12:1).

Satan knows that we are human and we have a tendency to be easily distracted. He just doesn't know how much distraction it will take to get you to throw your hands up and walk away from your promise. During my worst season, the enemy came against me from several directions. He attacked my son with addiction. My aunt died. He attacked my finances. I almost lost my home. He tried to break me. But it didn't work. I made the choice to push ahead. I was relentless in my pursuit of the promises.

I hunkered down for the storm, and I rode it out. I believed Isaiah 40:31 with all my heart: "But they that wait upon the Lord shall renew their strength; they shall mount up with wings as eagles; they shall run, and not be weary; and they shall walk, and not faint."

This was producing a harvest of endurance and strength. When we're fighting a spiritual battle we can expect pressure and challenges. But we should never give up. We must keep declaring the Word and believing "I am delivered." Be mindful that the enemy wants to steer you off course. Stay focused. Keep your mind stayed on Jesus. Declare the promise and know that if the enemy is trying desperately to get you off track, your breakthrough must be close.

FAITH DECLARATION

I endure and persevere.

*My mind is fixed. I am focused
on the things of God.*

*I keep my eyes on the Lord.
He perfects my faith.*

*I look forward to the manifestation
of God's promises.*

*I sing joyful praises. I lift my
hands in worship.*

I am pregnant with expectation.

My breakthrough is imminent.

DISCUSSION QUESTIONS

1. What types of distractions do you face in your daily spiritual walk or personal walk?

2. How do distractions affect spiritual growth and jeopardize your overall success?

3. What are some examples of distractions you've experienced or witnessed?

4. What happens when you take your focus off God's promises?

5. What are some ways to stay focused?

Chapter 7

THE FORMULA FOR MANIFESTATION

The Word is a force you cannot see, but you can
see the manifestation of that force, the expression
of the Word, which is your own life.
—MIGUEL ANGEL RUIZ

Years ago in a corporate setting, I was sharing with a coworker how I had just been diagnosed with high blood pressure. His immediate response was, "Be careful. You could stroke out and die."

At first I laughed it off. "Boy, you're so crazy." But later that day, I started thinking about what he said. It was true that extreme stress could increase blood pressure and even lead to a stroke. Had I been experiencing a little numbness—maybe even a little fatigue and dizziness? The negative thoughts started running rampant in my mind. Honestly, before hearing my friend's "words of wisdom"—emphasis on *dom*—having a stroke had never entered my mind. I meditated on his negativity, and voilà!

I started experiencing symptoms. Ever heard of hypochondria? *The American Century Dictionary* defines it as an abnormal anxiety about one's health. My grandmother was accused of being a hypochondriac. She was always experiencing multiple types of illnesses. Even though doctors couldn't find anything wrong, bottles of prescriptions lined her dresser. Eighty percent of her day was spent in bed. Granny only got out of the house for doctor's appointments. Friends and neighbors visited with their stories of doom and gloom. Their words were feeding her fear of death by illness. If only she had known the power that she had within her to speak health and healing into her life, to control her anxiety, and to call forth a sound mind and peace.

Granny had the fiery darts of negativity shooting at her from all directions—both from within and from the gloomy people around her. What's my point? She meditated on the thoughts, and like seeds, they took root and produced fear. The fear produced doubt, and doubt murders faith. The constant meditating on negativity led to her taking multiple medications, but never to her being healed. As believers we must not allow negativity to overcome us. Read Paul's instructions to the Church: "For the weapons of our warfare are not carnal, but mighty through God to the pulling down of strong holds; casting down imaginations, and every high thing that exalteth itself against the knowledge of God, and bringing into captivity every thought to the obedience of Christ" (2 Corinthians 10:4-5).

We have to capture bad thoughts and control them with the Word of God. The only way to win a spiritual battle is to fight it using spiritual weapons.

We are human, but we don't wage war as humans do. We use God's mighty weapons, not worldly weapons, to knock down the strongholds of human reasoning and to destroy false arguments (2 Corinthians 10:3-4 NLT).

If I hadn't come to myself and remembered that Jesus died that I might have life, I would have meditated my way right into a stroke. How could this happen?

Meditation + Declaration = Manifestation

It's a process. First, you see or hear something negative. Next, you think about it or meditate on it (too long). Then, you start speaking or declaring the negative thing you saw or heard. Finally, the negativity overcomes you and you begin to feel like there is no hope.

Here's an example. Say you're having relationship issues. Like most people, you want to vent. So you talk to your friends about your situation. More often than not, as your friends, they will take your side.

You hear your friends' words. You worry (meditate) about the negative aspects of your relationship. You start speaking negatively (declaration). Your relationship ends (manifestation).

They begin to say negative things about your situation like, "She's never going to change," "Just leave," or "You deserve better." All these seeds are planted in your mind, just waiting to be watered with fear so that they can grow and produce division and dissolution.

What you meditate on will manifest. That's why no matter how bad a situation gets, it's important to stay positive. God's Word encourages us to meditate on Scripture day and night (see Joshua 1:8).

Meditation

What we meditate on will eventually manifest in our lives. A quick search on the Internet will lead you to discover that many very successful people dedicate fifteen to twenty minutes a day just to meditate.

Society says meditation should be clearing the mind and thinking of nothing, but Scripture tells us in Psalm 1:2, "But his delight is in the law of the Lord; and on His law doth he meditate day and night," and Philippians 4:4-9 tells us to think on things that are good and pure.

So, yes, you want to take time to sit quietly; clear your mind of all impure and negative thoughts that are keeping you from God's best. Motivational speaker Les Brown said, "Cleaning is not just good for your house, it is healthy for your mind."

Take a moment to clear out the gunk so that you can then replace the brain-clogging thoughts with the Word of God. Whether you listen to a sermon, focus on a single scripture, or silently reflect on several memory verses. The goal is to fill your mind with the seeds of God's Word. Continually sow the Word into your mind, and allow it to germinate so that it takes and grows into your heart, increasing your faith. "Meditate upon these things; give thyself wholly to them; that thy profiting may appear to all" (1 Timothy 4:15).

The Word cannot take root without meditation, and without a strong root system, you will not be able to produce. So Paul encourages us to abide in His Word, and we will develop a strong spiritual root system. One that will support every blessing He has for us and will help us to win others to Christ, where they too can be delivered from the clutches of negativity.

Spending Time in Reflection

Instead of spending your time reading fiction novels, chatting online, or obsessing over social networking posts, spend some time with God. Get to know Him. Read His Word and seek His wisdom.

Some people get up early in the morning to pray. Others pray three times a day. There is no single "correct" method or process to get to know your God.

I find that getting up a little earlier in the morning to pray really does get my day started right. But, I admit, because I'm not a morning person, my study time is usually during lunch while my toddler is sleeping, or in the evenings. Start where you are. Don't feel like you have to get up at 6:00 A.M. every morning or read the entire Bible in ninety days. Start by reading a memory verse each morning and reflect on it.

Think about what the verse is saying and how it applies to your life. Ask God for revelation and understanding. The more you do this, the more you will understand who God is and what His plan is for you. This is your journey. Set your own pace. Read the Word. Meditate on it. Ask God for understanding and wisdom. You don't have to do what everyone else is doing. Do what works for you; but whatever you do, get started.

Here are four things to do when preparing to spend time with God:

1. Turn off the telephone or ringer. Trust me; the minute you get started praising, worshiping, reading your Bible, or meditating, the phone will ring. Turn it off.

2. Lock the door to your room if you are able. This prevents someone unexpectedly walking in to ask you about lost car keys or to complain that a favorite toy is missing.

3. Make it known. Let people in your house know that you are designating time to spend with God, and that you should not be interrupted.

4. Have everything you need handy. Be sure your pen, favorite Bible, worship CD, journal, or anything else you think you will need during this time is near at hand. You don't want to have to go the car to get your Bible in the middle of your meditation.

Spending time with God strengthens your relationship with Him. Any relationship suffers when the parties involved don't devote quality time to sustain the bond between them.

Sit Still and Listen

My prayers used to be microwave conversations with God. I put in my request, went round and round about how I felt about the issue, and when I was done, I popped up and proceeded to the next task. My prayers were quick, fast, and hurried. There was no time allocated to "listening," only time dedicated to asking.

I had a million reasons why I didn't have time to sit still and listen after praying. I was tired; I was sleepy. I had laundry to wash, calls to return, and dinner to cook. My son needed help with his homework, or my friend needed advice. Asking for help with my bills and a new promotion at work was higher on my priority list than listening. I asked. He listened. I pleaded. He listened some more. Then, when I was done, prayer time was over. At that point, I figured it was up to Him to work it out.

I'd missed it. Prayer is communication. Communication involves dialoguing and listening. You talk, God listens. Then God talks, and you listen. I think many people, like me, get so caught up in asking, that we forget to listen for the answer.

God answers in many ways. He speaks through music, songs, Scripture, dreams, ideas, and so on. Sometimes as you sit silently, God may provoke a thought or gently urge you to read a particular scripture. Take time to hear what He has to say. Hear with your heart, and hear with your mind. You'll be glad you did.

Listen to Praise Music

Music has been found to have an effect on the thinking process, and it can affect the listener's mood. Research shows that listening to positive music makes it easier for people to perform difficult tasks.

If you find yourself in an odd place and don't have access to music, sing a song instead. Paul and Silas sang songs and praised God while they were locked in prison! The foundations started shaking, and the shackles fell off.

Whatever the prison you are bound in, if you just sing praises to the Lord, I promise you that God will move and release you from your bondage. No jail cell or shackle can hold you. God has the master key. So don't sit there and mope and sulk like I used to do. Get up, turn on some praise music, and dance like David did!

By meditating in the Word day and night we are nurturing the Word and giving it the right conditions to take root and to begin to produce fruit in our lives. Only then will we be able to stand strong and come out victorious in every storm of life. Your Bible is a book full of seeds. You have two choices. You can plant those seeds in your heart every day or place your Bible on the mantle for decoration.

When I was working to regrow my lawn, some days it seemed nothing was happening, but I knew the grass seeds were working beneath the ground. Likewise, though it seemed my son's behavior was getting worse, I knew God was working. I kept the faith. I knew that calling him names, yelling, and condemning him would not help him, nor would it make me feel good either. I knew that I'd sown, and I was expecting to reap. "Train up a child in the way he should go: and when he is old, he will not depart from it" (Proverbs 22:6). The Word is an incorruptible seed, meaning it cannot be destroyed and it will produce if you sow it, protect it, and expect the harvest.

Try these meditation techniques:

1. Find a quiet place to sit or lie in a relaxed position.

2. Breathe regularly and relax.

3. Stop thinking about all the negative things that are happening.

4. Concentrate your thoughts upon Scripture, spiritual music, poetry, or personal faith declaration. Give it your full attention.

5. If some negative image or thought pops into your head, stop it, and go back to the object of meditation.

These steps will help you renew your mind, if done consistently. Remember, don't allow old negative thought patterns to remain, giving the enemy ammunition to drag you deeper into distress. This will only reinforce negative self-talk. Replace negative thoughts with higher level thinking—God thoughts. What you put in your mind will determine what comes out of your mouth and the cycle will continue.

Meditating on a Specific Principle or Promise

Find a scripture that pertains to your situation. If you need deliverance, search for deliverance scriptures. If you need a financial breakthrough, search for prosperity, abundance, and charity verses. For your relationships with family and friends, search for scriptures about unity, love, and togetherness.

Several years ago when my home was facing foreclosure and my then-teenage son was rebelling in every way imaginable, I meditated on the Word. I didn't just choose random scriptures. I searched for verses that pertained to the challenges that I was facing. I began with the concordance in my Bible. I searched for words like *favor*, *children*, and *victory*. Some of the scriptures I remembered from sermons and lessons I'd heard in the past. Others were new to me. I read, "the seed of the righteous shall be delivered" (Proverbs 11:21). I declared it and I meditated on it daily.

For every problem you face, God has a promise of deliverance readily available. You have to be willing to seek if you want to find. Grab your Bible or tablet and start searching. Find out what the Scripture says about your circumstance. "Ask, and it shall be given you; seek, and ye shall find; knock, and it shall be opened unto you" (Matthew 7:7). There is no substitute for studying the Bible and receiving inspiration from the Holy Spirit. It's an awesome feeling when you read a scripture that speaks directly to your heart. The words come alive, and you feel inspired and uplifted almost instantly. It's the hope you receive from Scripture that will help carry you during your weakest moments.

Declaration

The definition of *declaration* is a verbal statement of your intentions or purpose. When we verbally articulate the Word of God, we are announcing to the world, "This is who God says I am, and this is what I choose to believe." Remember, we said earlier that your intentions and beliefs reside in your heart. When we speak, we reveal those intentions. If you spend time meditating, studying, and praying, the Word will change your mind. It will influence your beliefs, and your self-talk will go from negative to positive.

Declare what you desire, not what you detest. When we choose to declare the Word of God, even though things aren't going well, we are setting our faith wheels in motion. As we confess, we are showing that we believe in our hearts that God's Word is powerful enough to exact change.

Declare, "The Lord Will Deliver"

> *If it be so, our God whom we serve is able to deliver us from the burning fiery furnace, and He will deliver us out of thine hand, O king* (Daniel 3:17).

In the midst of their horrible circumstances, the Hebrew boys chose to remain faithful. If they'd bowed, their lives would have been spared. But they had so much faith in the power of God that they stood firm and declared, "Our God is able to deliver us."

They believed that God would deliver them out of the enemy's clutches. But an even greater show of faith was the statement they made immediately following, in verse 18: "But if not, be it known unto thee, O king, that we will not serve thy gods, nor worship the golden image which thou hast set up." I don't believe this statement indicates in any way that they doubted God. I believe they were simply saying, "Whatever God chooses to allow, we will accept that." Only God knows what thoughts flooded their minds as they watched the guard turn up the furnace ten times hotter. It had to be a horrifying experience—one that many would have bowed to under pressure and done anything to get out of facing the fire. Yet still, on the verge of being pushed in, the Hebrew boys declared deliverance.

God has promised to deliver us from every affliction (see Psalm 34:19). Stand firm on His promise. Don't bow under the pressure of negative thoughts and emotions. Know that God desires only the best for you. Even if the situation doesn't turn out the way you think it should, know that God is right in there with you and everything is going to work out in your favor. Ignore the negative self-chatter that's telling you you're going to fail, you're going to die. Do what the Hebrew boys did. Push those thoughts out of your mind. Don't be distracted by how bad it seems. Stand firm and declare by faith, "The Lord will deliver!"

Declare His Marvelous Works

"Declare His glory among the heathen; His marvellous works among all nations. For great is the Lord, and greatly to be praised" (1 Chronicles 16:24-25). Be an instrument of praise. Use your words to proclaim to the world that God is awesome.

Lift up your heads, O ye gates; and be ye lift up, ye everlasting doors; and the King of glory shall come in. Who is this King of glory? The Lord strong and mighty, the Lord mighty in battle (Psalm 24:7-8).

God deserves our praise. It may seem that praising someone else isn't the best way to stay motivated and encouraged, but when it comes to your almighty God—your Savior, Provider, Banner, and Protector—it's a different story. You can't help but be lifted up yourself! It's the powerful by-product of lifting your hands in adoration to the mighty Father. When you do, you stop declaring your feelings and circumstances. Instead, you come into the presence of God; and, in His presence, fear, anger, loss, doubt, and, yes, negative self-talk must flee.

There was a time in my life when I suffered from depression. I was so down that I had to make myself get out of bed and go to church on Sunday mornings. I felt tired and worn out. My heart was heavy, but when I lifted my hands during praise and worship, something happened. The stress lifted. You see, when we glorify God and lift Him up, the devil flees because he hates praise. When the joy of the Lord takes hold of you, you feel stronger, healthier, and happier. "For ye shall go out with joy and be led forth with peace: the mountains and the hills shall break forth before you into singing, and all the trees of the field shall clap their hands" (Isaiah 55:12). Now that's praise.

Praising God and declaring His goodness will lift you up. His everlasting, loving arms will envelop you as you stand in His presence. You don't have to be a professional speaker, singer, or have the perfect stance or swagger. Just turn up some praise music and lift your hands to the heavens. Give

Him the praise He is due, and be lifted up into a realm of joy, hope, love, and ever-increasing faith. Let Him take control. Don't let your problems get you down. Look to the heavens from which your help comes (see Psalm 121:1). Praise the Lord with all your heart, and declare His marvelous works, and watch your deliverance spring forth!

Declare That You Are Delivered

When David faced Goliath, he shouted, "Thou comest to me with a sword, and with a spear, and with a shield: but I come to thee in the name of the Lord of hosts, the God of the armies of Israel" (1 Samuel 17:45). Your problems and challenges are no match for the Lord of Hosts. You must believe with all your heart and never doubt that God would deliver you, just like David believed that his God would deliver him from Goliath. No matter how big the giant or how many people are telling you that the giant is too big to conquer, stand and declare victory. Put on your spiritual armor, plant your victory banner, and continue to pray without ceasing. Let these words encourage you as you claim your victory over negativity: "Be strong and of a good courage; be not afraid, neither be thou dismayed: for the Lord thy God is with thee whithersoever thou goest" (Joshua 1:9). Stand on this verse, speak it, and during your daily activities give your burdens to the Lord.

There is a song we used to sing when I was younger. The chorus encouraged, "Turn it over to Jesus. He can work it out." We have to have faith to believe that God will solve everything. That He is faithful to deliver us from every affliction (see Psalm 34:19). Really give the situation over to Him. Ask Him, "Lord, would you please carry this burden for me as you promised you would?" If God promised, He will do it. He is not a man that He should lie—ever. Lift your burdens up to Him. "Lord, I don't know the answer. I can't bear this any longer." His grace is sufficient for you, as His strength is made perfect in weakness (see 2 Corinthians 12:9). When you are weak, He is strong. There is no Goliath too big or too strong. The Lord of Hosts is with you. Declare, *I am delivered!*

Manifestation

Our thoughts and words create outcomes. Those outcomes are called manifestations. Look around you. Everything that you see is a manifestation of someone's thoughts. However, none of what you see appeared overnight. It took some time, and so will the manifestation of God's word in your life. Yes, God can miraculously deliver you from whatever enslaves you, but most of the time there is a process. Step by step we grow, learn, and change. The seed of the Word is sown into our minds and takes root, spreading to our hearts and budding in our speech. You have to work the process and keep at it even if it gets tough. If you make a mistake, don't quit. Start again.

It's human nature to want to quit. By not following your nature, you're walking by faith. Though it may seem that the desired results aren't manifesting and your work is all for nothing, stay diligent. Keep pushing forward, standing firm on the victory that you have already obtained through Christ Jesus.

Your Persistence Is a Must

And He spake a parable unto them to this end, that men ought always to pray, and not to faint (Luke 18:1).

In Luke 18, verses 1-8, Jesus tells the disciples the story of a widow woman who was very persistent in her pursuit to obtain justice from a certain judge. Jesus shared this parable with the disciples to encourage them that they should continue to pray and never give up.

What's interesting about the judge in Luke 18 is that he was an unbeliever. The scripture says that he "neither feared God nor cared about people" (NLT). Many times in life we are dealing with people who couldn't care less about our situations. Yet because they are in positions of authority, we are forced to have to deal with them anyway. As believers, we should not be afraid to face these kinds of people, because we have a God who can turn the cold hearts of men and give us favor in every situation. Though the judge did not grant the widow justice the first time she requested it, she did not give up and walk away without hope. Instead, she returned to the judge again and again.

There are times when it seems that our request is being ignored. We pray and pray, but no answer—no results. This is not the time to tuck tail and walk away. Instead, this is a time to press in and stand firm. Because the widow woman did not give up and she was persistent in the pursuit of justice for her case, the judge granted her justice. It's important to note that the judge did not grant the widow justice because he cared about her or because he was a man of God with compassion. The judge gave her what she wanted because she was persistent. There is power in persistence. If an unrighteous judge can grant a petition, surely our God who loves us dearly will grant our petition as well.

Though it seems the promises are not manifesting in your life, don't give up. Keep praying and keep going before Him with your requests. Read Luke 18 for encouragement. Remain in faith that you will receive justice and your petition will be granted. In the dictionary, *persistence* is defined as firm or obstinate continuance in a course of action in spite of difficulty or opposition. Whether the request is for business success, a family matter, or a health concern, stay your course of faith regardless of the difficulty you face. Keep going before God with a good attitude. He loves you and hears your cry. But you must not give up. Your faith and persistence have power.

Sometimes Challenges Arise Just before Your Manifestation

A woman's water breaks and labor begins as the blessing of a child begins to push forth out of the womb into the world for all to see. Every breakthrough cycle has a breaking point. As the break happens and the change begins, things may seem far worse. We may lose friends. Our health may take a turn for the worse. Our business may look like it's going under. Or, as in my case, a child may go astray. The breaking point isn't the time to give up; it's the time to dig in. It's a sign that your manifestation is on its way. The pressure is mounting. The Word that you've sown into your life is changing your environment. It's making preparation to take root, creating an environment that will sustain your blessing long term. I reflected over many years of trials and triumphs, and I realized that the times that I succeeded were the times that I didn't give up when things looked bad. I stuck with it and I pushed past the pain.

Sowing the Word and expecting a manifestation is like that. We get past the stages of clearing clutter from our hearts and declaring the Word from our lips, but then comes the really challenging part—waiting. During the waiting stage, the enemy plants doubt and fear. If we're not careful, we will clog our hearts again and choke out the Word that we've worked so diligently to believe—we will stop believing. We will start doubting. When we begin to doubt, we lose faith, and we never see our promise come to pass, because we give up during the most critical stage of the process—the waiting stage.

Satan knows that we are human and we have a tendency to give up under pressure. He just doesn't know how much pressure it will take to get you to give up. For me, he piled on my son's rebellion. He piled on the denial of my modification request. He piled on people gossiping about me. He was trying to make me break down. This time I didn't. I hunkered down for the storm, and I was ready to ride it out. Isaiah 40:31 was rooted in my heart: "But they that wait upon the Lord shall renew their strength; they shall mount up with wings as eagles; they shall run, and not be weary; and they shall walk, and not faint." This was producing a harvest of endurance and strength. I expected pressure. I expected challenges. I embraced them as a prelude to my breakthrough. The Word was breaking forth; it was taking root and making changes. Moreover, those changes were in my favor. Victory was on the way.

FAITH DECLARATION

*Today I am thankful. I have a
grateful heart, and I am content.*

I am at peace, and forgiveness floods my heart.

*I only desire what God has for me,
and I am open to receive it.*

God's favor abounds toward me.

*I patently await the magnificent
manifestation of God's blessings to
come upon me and overtake me.*

Any day now I will reap if I faint not.

DISCUSSION QUESTIONS

1. How important is meditating on the Word?

2. What's your favorite form of meditation? How do you currently meditate?

3. What do you think is the most difficult part of the manifestation formula (meditating, declaring, or waiting for manifestation)?

4. What is your favorite time of day to spend with God? What do you do during that time?

5. How do you avoid distractions during your meditation time?

6. How often should we as believers declare the Word over our lives? How often do you (all day, weekly, not very often)?

7. What does manifestation mean to you?

Chapter 8

WHAT ARE YOU SAYING ABOUT YOURSELF?

Never say anything about yourself you
do not want to come true.
—BRIAN TRACY

When bills are piling up and you have more month than money, it can be easy to get discouraged. That discouragement often is so pressing that we begin to vent about our problems to the people around us. Whether they are close friends, coworkers, family members, or the teller at the bank, we have to remember that our first point of contact should always be God.

Reaching out for help when you need it is smart, but we should never place our complete confidence in human beings. Instead, we should seek help and guidance from the Lord first. Sometimes in times of turmoil we act too quickly; and, out of frustration, we share our struggles with friends, family, and coworkers in hopes that they will "solve" our problem.

While it is great to have someone to confide in, sometimes in our stress we do not choose our confidants wisely. We leave ourselves open to individuals who either do not have our best interests at heart or, worse, may betray confidence. The Bible instructs us to seek wise counsel. If you must share, be sure that it is with someone who lives by godly principles.

God has blessed us with fellowship, but our faith and trust should always be founded in our Lord. Know that He will, sometimes through other people, help us to overcome what we are faced with because He promised to do so. The key is to seek Him first, not last. Allow God to bring the right people into your path, and know that whether He works through someone or performs a miracle—it will all be so that He will get the glory.

Then and only then will our situation glorify God and encourage other people to seek Him as well. God wants to help you. He wants to show Himself strong in your time of weakness so that the Kingdom of God will be glorified and others will be blessed through your situation.

God Cares What You Call Yourself

God is serious about what we call ourselves. Names have meanings and power. It may seem innocent to call yourself stupid, dumb, ignorant, or inadequate. But those are not names that you should ever use to describe yourself. These names eat away at your self-esteem and threaten to lower your self-worth.

When God told *Abram* (meaning "exalted father") he would become the father of many nations, he changed his name to *Abraham* ("father of many nations") (Genesis 17:5).

When *Sarai* ("princess") was promised a child, her name was changed to *Sarah* ("my princess") (Genesis 17:15).

I find the story of Naomi interesting. Naomi and her daughter-in-law both experienced great loss. Naomi lost her husband and her two sons. Ruth lost her husband and was now alone and virtually destitute. Here you have two women whose lives were shaken to the core. While they both had similar trials individually, we see in Scripture that they approached the situation with very different attitudes.

Naomi was so distressed by her disappointments that she renamed herself Mara, meaning bitter. In her mind she believed that God was the reason for her misfortune.

> *And she said unto them, Call me not Naomi, call me Mara: for the Almighty hath dealt very bitterly with me. I went out full and the Lord hath brought me home again empty: why then call ye me Naomi, seeing the Lord hath testified against me, and the Almighty hath afflicted me?* (Ruth 1:20-21)

Instead of keeping her given name, which meant *pleasantness* or *happiness*, she began to call herself *bitter*.

Isn't that unfortunate? She had a beautiful name that foretold happiness, but she ditched it and instructed everyone to call her bitter instead. A lot of us today are following suit. We are allowing the enemy to deceive us into believing that God is causing misfortune in our lives. We've resolved to walk around bitter, and everyone around us knows it.

We are calling ourselves bitter, angry, sad—names that God never meant for us to have. I don't want to go down the derogatory names road, but so many of our youth are watching videos and reality television and thinking that it's okay to be called by names other than their given names, and what's worse is they are calling one another by these names.

Satan is a deceiver. He wants you to believe that God is hurting you so that you will forsake your identity in Christ and strip away the power that belongs to you in the name of Jesus. He wants you to dismiss the importance of what you call yourself so that you talk yourself into depression, loneliness, and despair. He wants you to tell yourself that you are nothing, but that is a lie. Read Ephesians 2:10 for inspiration: "For we are God's masterpiece. He has created us anew in Christ Jesus, so we can do the good things He planned for us long ago" (NLT). God's word is clear. You are a masterpiece!

Naomi, even though she served the living God, mistakenly believed that she had nothing to live for. Many people today feel that their lives are over because they have gone through some turmoil or lost someone they loved dearly. They're hurting and believe that God wants them to suffer and has dealt them a bad hand, so they give up and live life bitter.

But Ruth offers us an example of hope. She approached the situation in a different way. Scripture says Naomi tried to encourage her two daughters-in-law, Orpah and Ruth, to return to their families. But only one, Orpah, went away crying and depressed. Ruth, on the other hand, clung to Naomi, begging her to let her go with her to Israel.

Ruth had lost everything. She probably thought, "What have I got to lose? I'm going for it." Even though Naomi was negative about her own circumstances, Ruth didn't let Naomi's wavering faith and pessimistic attitude dissuade her from leaving the past behind and believing for a better future.

The interesting fact is, in her past Ruth served pagan gods. She didn't have the same God as Naomi, but she still recognized the power of Naomi's God and wanted to serve Him. Ruth adopted the right attitude—an attitude of faith. Once in Israel, Ruth didn't sit idle, hoping and wishing that God would do something for her. Instead, she began to work in the fields. Her life was full. She was caring for her mother-in-law, Naomi, worshiping her new God, and earning her keep working in the fields (see Ruth 2:2). It was while she was living her life pleasing God that she met Boaz and found favor.

Let Ruth's example encourage you. Decide right now that you want to create a more positive life for yourself and the people you love. You have the influence, God gave you the power, and now the choice is yours. Will you be afraid, or will you begin a new life by faith? You can start anew. God's favor is waiting for you in your future.

When we remain positive and put our trust in God, He is faithful to bless us. It may not happen overnight, but it will happen. Whatever the situation in your life, He can improve it, but He needs you to be persistent in your faith. He needs you to close your mind to the negativity around you and the deceitful lies of the enemy. Then you will see the Lord work in your life, and His favor will abound. Letting our lives become a testimony, we encourage other women to stay positive as well.

God loves you immensely. In John 15:15 God calls you *friend*. Then, in Firsat John 3:1, He calls you His child. You are a new creature in Second Corinthians 5:17, and in Psalm 139:14 David said, "I am fearfully and wonderfully made." Know who you are and whose you are. You are a friend of God, and you are fearfully and wonderfully made.

PERSONAL SPEAKING GUIDE

- **Don't say:** I can't do that. I'm too scared. What if I fail?
- **Do say:** I am courageous. God has not given me a spirit of fear, but of a sound mind, power, and love.

- **Don't say:** I'm always broke.
- **Do say:** I am abundantly supplied. God is supplying all of my needs according to His riches in glory.

- **Don't say:** I am so depressed.
- **Do say:** I have the mind of Christ and the peace of God that surpasses all understanding.

- **Don't say:** I just can't stop this bad habit.
- **Do say:** I am not tempted or tried above that which I am able to overcome. I am more than a conqueror.

- **Don't say:** Everyone in my family has this problem. It's hereditary, so I will probably have the same problems too.
- **Do say:** Christ redeemed me from the curse, being made a curse Himself. I am delivered out of every affliction.

- **Don't say:** I don't like people. I'd rather be alone; besides, people are mean.

- **Do say:** I have the compassion of Christ in my heart, and I love all people.

- **Don't say:** I'll never meet this deadline. My work is overwhelming me; there's no way that I can meet the demands of this job.

- **Do say:** I have the grace to overcome every obstacle. God is giving me wisdom to solve every problem that I am faced with.

- **Don't say:** I'm happy with what I have. Why should I want more?

- **Do say:** Jesus came that I might have abundant life. I am blessed to be a blessing to others.

- **Don't say:** I will never get married. No one wants to marry me.

- **Do say:** God is preparing me for marriage, and He is raising up the perfect mate for me.

- **Don't say:** God is not answering my prayers so maybe He's not listening.

- **Do say:** God is mindful of me, and He hears me when I pray.

- **Don't say:** Everything is getting on my nerves, and I am going crazy!

- **Do say:** I will think only of things that are lovely, good, just, and have good report so that the peace of God dwells in me.

- **Don't say:** I'm so angry. I will never be able to forgive.

- **Do say:** The joy of the Lord is my strength. My heart is filled with the compassion of Christ, and I forgive those who trespass against me.

- **Don't say:** My company is going to have a reduction in force. I don't know what I'm going to do if I get laid off.
- **Do say:** When one door closes, God has to open another door.

- **Don't say:** I am lonely. I wish I had someone to in my life.
- **Do say:** I am complete in Christ. I am never lonely because He is always with me.

- **Don't say:** Things will never get better. I may as well give up.
- **Do say:** Eyes haven't seen what God has prepared for me, and in due season I shall reap if I faint not.

- **Don't say:** The weather is terrible. I hope I don't have an accident.
- **Do say:** The angels of the Lord are encamped around me, and no hurt or harm shall come near me.

- **Don't say:** I'm too old to change. You can't teach old dogs new tricks.
- **Do say:** I am a new creature. Old things have passed away.

- **Don't say:** Everyone else is doing it; why shouldn't I?
- **Do say:** God has called me out of darkness and into His marvelous light. I am in this world, but I am not of this world.

- **Don't say:** I can't help gossiping. My friends encourage it.
- **Do say:** I will not participate in gossip. Corrupt communication brings destruction.

- **Don't say:** No one cares about me!
- **Do say:** God loves me and He is Jehovah-Shammah ("the Lord is there").

DISCUSSION QUESTIONS

1. What are some of the negative words you've used to describe yourself?

2. Have you ever found yourself in a situation similar to Naomi or Ruth? How did you handle the pressure?

3. Have you ever accused God of causing your problem? Do you believe that God is responsible for the problems that we face? Why or why not?

4. What can we learn from Ruth's example? How did her approach differ from Naomi's?

5. Why do you think most people give up and become negative at the first sign of struggle or adversity?

Chapter 9

WHAT ARE YOU SAYING ABOUT OTHERS?

*Before you speak ask yourself if what you are
going to say is true, is kind, is necessary, is
helpful. If the answer is no, maybe what you
are about to say should be left unsaid.*
—BERNARD MELTZER

During my aunt's battle with breast cancer, I would tell her constantly, "Don't talk yourself out of your healing." Maybe you're in a similar situation. Someone you love dearly is ill, and you feel helpless to do anything. You may not be able to take away their pain or make their disease go away, but you can pray and stand in faith with them.

I watched an interesting documentary once that showed how people who had others praying for them healed faster than those who were going through their illness alone. "The effectual fervent prayer of a righteous man availeth much" (James 5:16). Sickness and disease often progress over a period of time, and often the healing process is progressive as well. Don't be discouraged if you lay hands on someone and there is no immediate physical indication of healing. This reminds me of Jesus cursing the tree and commanding the roots to dry up. At that moment, nothing visibly changed about the tree. That's because the change started beneath the ground in the roots—invisible to the eye. The next time they passed, the tree was dead. That is what I believe about some sickness and disease. Prayer begins to work when we believe. We may not see it, but we must believe it in order to receive. "And all things, whatsoever ye shall ask in prayer, believing, ye shall receive" (Matthew 21:22).

Be Supportive

Let all bitterness, and wrath, and anger, and clamour, and evil speaking, be put away from you, with all malice: and be ye kind one to another, tenderhearted, forgiving one another, even as God for Christ's sake hath forgiven you" (Ephesians 4:31-32).

When someone you know is going through a challenge, be supportive. When they are down, lift them up. Don't share negative experiences; share positive ones. Don't bombard them with your Internet research on death statistics; share healing testimonies and research successful new innovations.

Do whatever you can to help them enter into a place of rest, to be at peace. My aunt used to tell me that she loved for me to visit because she always felt better after I left. People should feel better when you leave them. They shouldn't feel drained.

I'm not trying to make you feel bad. I just want you to be aware that your words matter. The things that you are saying could be hurting your loved ones' chances of experiencing the healing they've been praying for.

God's favor and grace should shine through in your words, actions, and attitude. They shouldn't see you distraught, in tears, and hopeless. By all means, they should never feel as though you have given up on them. I knew a lady who was visited in the hospital by a few church members. She said during the visit they started asking her questions about the type of program she wanted at her funeral!

Our words should always agree with the Word of God. Regardless of how bad things look or how difficult the situation, we should always be loving, supportive, and faithful. During the critical moments of a person's life, we must be sure that we are speaking life, not death (see Proverbs 18:21).

> Most of us, swimming against the tides of trouble the world knows nothing about, need only a bit of praise or encouragement—and we will make the goal.
>
> —JEROME FLEISHMAN

PERSONAL SPEAKING GUIDE

- **Don't say:** My supervisor hates me; my coworkers are messy. I hate this job!
- **Do say:** I love those who hate me, and I will do well to those who misuse me. No weapon formed against me shall prosper. The battle is the Lord's.

- **Don't say:** My children do not listen to a word that I say. They are just bad.
- **Do say:** My children are a blessing from the Lord. My children obey the Word of God and honor their mother and father.

- **Don't say:** My husband is lazy and worthless. I don't know why I married him.
- **Do say:** My husband is a righteous man of God, and he loves me like Christ loves the Church.

- **Don't say:** My in-laws are incorrigible and they are making my life miserable.
- **Do say:** My in-laws are transformed by the renewing of their minds. I am an example for them, and they will see my good works and glorify the Father in Heaven.

- **Don't say:** People in church are cruel. I'm never going to church again.

- **Do say:** God has many great churches, and He is revealing to me the church that I should attend.

- **Don't say:** My child makes terrible grades in school. They will never amount to anything.
- **Do say:** God has a purpose for my child. My child is a royal priesthood and has the wisdom of Daniel and the favor of God and man. My child is empowered to prosper.

- **Don't say:** Why do they behave that way? They're just crazy.
- **Do say:** Christ alone is perfect.

- **Don't say:** Yeah, right! There's no cure for what you have.
- **Do say:** I agree with you in Jesus's name, by His stripes you are healed and made whole (see Matthew 18:19).

- **Don't say:** You're only going to get worse.
- **Do say:** The Lord is restoring health to you. He is healing your (heart, mind, body, etc.) (see Jeremiah 30:17).

- **Don't say:** The doctor said you're never going to (walk, talk, see, etc.) again.
- **Do say:** You can do all things through Christ who strengthens your (legs, arms, eyes, mind, etc.) (see Philippians 4:13).

- **Don't say:** God must be punishing you for something.
- **Do say:** God loves you. You are forgiven, and by His stripes you are healed (see 1 Peter 2:24).

- **Don't say:** They have one foot in the grave.
- **Do say:** The same Spirit that raised Christ from the dead lives in you and is strengthening your physical body (see Romans 8:11).

DISCUSSION QUESTIONS

1. Can you remember a time when you had to be supportive of someone else during a difficult time in his or her life? How did you handle that? What did you say?

2. Have you ever said something discouraging to another person, and later you felt bad about what you said? What happened?

3. What types of words should we avoid when talking to people who are facing health challenges?

4. Have you ever been inspired by something that someone said to you? What did they say? How did you feel?

5. What do you think you should say or do when you're not sure of the right words to say?

Chapter 10

WHAT ARE OTHERS SAYING ABOUT YOU?

Don't be trapped by dogma—which is living with the results of other people's thinking. Don't let the noise of others' opinions drown out your own inner voice. And most important have the courage to follow your heart and intuition.
—STEVE JOBS

God be true, but every man a liar.
—ROMANS 3:4

I was so angry when my aunt shared that her nurse told her she would never walk again. My aunt was terribly upset. Though she had no sensation from her hips down, she believed she would walk again. She'd believed so strongly that she allowed her son to help her with therapeutic exercises. She'd made plans for planting new rose bushes and reestablishing her garden. But after the nurse told her emphatically that those things would never happen, Auntie stopped believing.

She didn't say she no longer believed, but I could hear it in her words, "Why do the exercises if I'm never going to walk again?" The nurse's words of unbelief had been sown into her mind and had taken root. I beg you, do not allow the negative words of others to discourage you from believing in God's promises for your life. Your goal is always to speak life and not death. But sometimes it's not just your words that you have to be careful of. Sometimes other people will poison your faith with their negativity and pessimism. But you have power. You have favor. You have Jesus. Don't give up! "I have set before you life and death...choose life" (Deuteronomy 30:19). Choose to live!

You have the power of choice. Make the decision to be healed. You have to choose life. It's not just a default response. Our human nature tends to lean toward the negative. Choose life. "Death and life are in the power of the tongue" (Proverbs 18:21). You have power to call those "things that be not" as though they were. Use it to claim your healing and proclaim that Jesus is Lord of your life. Use your power to praise God for the healing He has promised you. Use the power of your tongue to rejoice in the face of adversity, to show the enemy that you will not give up on God; because God is mindful of you, and He has not given up on you. Amen!

PERSONAL SPEAKING GUIDE

- **They say:** You poor thing.
- **You say:** I am blessed, and I have the grace to overcome anything!

- **They say:** How do you plan to acquire that? You don't make enough.
- **You say:** I am abundantly supplied. I am not moved by what I see. It's only temporary.

- **They say:** That's a terrible sickness; you could die from it.
- **You say:** I am healed. I shall live and not die.

- **They say:** You don't look well. Are you sick?
- **You say:** I have divine health. I resist sickness in the name of Jesus.

- **They say:** Yeah, right—do you really believe you're going to pull that off?
- **You say:** I can do all things through Christ who strengthens me.

- **They say:** If I were you, I would be so depressed.
- **You say:** God has not given me the spirit of fear, but of a sound mind, power, and love.

- **They say:** I could never give that much money to the church. I have bills to pay.

- **You say:** When I give, God causes men to give to me—a good measure, pressed down, shaken together, and running over. God supplies all of my needs according to His riches in glory.

- **They say:** I don't believe in anything that I can't see.
- **You say:** Without faith it is impossible to please God. I receive the promise of God through faith.

- **They say:** Don't you get tired of cooking, cleaning, and taking care of everyone else?
- **You say:** I have the grace to care for the family God has blessed me with.

- **They shouldn't say:** What exactly did the doctor say is wrong with you?
- **They should say:** No weapon formed against you shall prosper. I'm standing in agreement with you for your healing (see Isaiah 54:17).

- **They shouldn't say:** You've been sick a long time. You're really bad off.
- **They should say:** God is restoring you and making you strong (see 1 Peter 5:10).

- **They shouldn't say:** You should just accept it (illness).
- **They should say:** I believe you are loosed from (illness) in Jesus's name (see Luke 13:12).

POSITIVE SPEAKING GUIDE

- **Don't say:** My entire body aches. I'm just falling apart!
- **Do say:** Sickness and disease shall not lord over me.

- **Don't say:** I am so exhausted. I really don't feel like doing anything today.
- **Do say:** I can do all things through Christ who strengthens me.

- **Don't say:** This headache is killing me!
- **Do say:** Headache, I resist you in the name of Jesus, and by His stripes I am healed and made whole.

- **Don't say:** I'm going to die.
- **Do say:** I shall live and declare the works of the Lord (see Psalm 118:17).

- **Don't say:** My health is getting worse.
- **Do say:** I am a believer and not a doubter. I believe I am healed no matter what I am experiencing (see Hebrews 11:1).

- **Don't say:** There's an epidemic; I'm probably going to catch it.
- **Do say:** I have the authority to overcome the power of the enemy. No epidemic shall harm me (see Luke 10:19).

- **Don't say:** My high blood pressure; my diabetes; my cancer.
- **Do say:** The Lord is removing from me all sickness and disease (see Deuteronomy 7:15).

- **Don't say:** This job is going to give me a heart attack!
- **Do say:** I work for the glory of God, not man. My work will be rewarded (see Colossians 3:23).

- **Don't say:** These children are going to be the death of me.
- **Do say:** The grace of God is in me. My children arise and call me blessed (see Romans 16:20; Proverbs 31:28).

- **Don't say:** I will never be whole again.
- **Do say:** My mind, body, and soul are restored and I am made whole by the power of Jesus through faith.

- **Don't say:** The treatments aren't working and there is nothing else the doctors can do.
- **Do say:** By His stripes I am healed. It is the Lord who heals me (see Exodus 15:26; Isaiah 53:5).

- **Don't say:** God hasn't healed me yet. Maybe healing is not for me.
- **Do say:** The Lord is full of compassion and mercy, and I patiently expect a total healing (see James 5:10-11).

DISCUSSION QUESTIONS

1. Can you remember a time when someone you thought supported you said something that discouraged you? How did you respond to them?

2. Have you ever been discouraged by something that someone else said to you? What happened?

3. Have you ever been inspired by something that someone said to you? What did they say? How did you feel?

4. When someone is constantly being negative in your presence, how do you address the issue in a positive way?

Chapter 11

THE POWER OF PERFECT LOVE

There will always be someone willing to hurt
you, put you down, gossip about you, belittle your
accomplishments, and judge your soul. It is a fact
that we all must face. However, if you realize
that God is a best friend that stands beside you
when others cast stones you will never be afraid,
never feel worthless, and never feel alone.
—SHANNON L. ALDER

I used to wonder if God would ever forgive me for my sins and transgressions. I must have asked and re-asked a million times in prayer, "Father, forgive me." I didn't understand that once I asked, He'd forgiven me and that was the end of it. I didn't know Psalm 103:12 that said, "As far as the east is from the west, so far hath He removed our transgressions from us."

Sure, I knew that God was a loving and forgiving God, but my sins seemed so big. Surely, I thought, the enormity of my sins required some extra groveling on my part. Truth is: There is nothing we can do to pardon our own sin. The intimate knowledge of God's love gives us the confidence to call those "things that be not" as though they were. When we understand He loves us unconditionally, we aren't afraid to go boldly to Him for help. We trust that His Word is true and His promises irrefutable. Most important, we understand that we don't have to be perfect to be blessed. The faith you use when you use God-speak is not your own. It's the Father's faith that you are using. That should encourage you to speak boldly and with the assurance that what you say will come to pass.

We are not perfect. Sometimes we miss the mark. "For all have sinned, and come short of the glory of God" (Romans 3:23). When I thought I was going to lose my home, I was afraid. But I could still feel God's arms of love. He reassured me that, no matter what, He would always be there for me. Though I had experienced homelessness in the past, He was doing a new thing, and homelessness was not a part of that plan. He was right by my side, and He would never leave me nor forsake me.

God saved my house. He brought my son back home. Not because I was a perfect Christian who was living a perfect life, but because I am His child, and His love for me is unconditional and everlasting. But even if I'd lost my home, I still would have faith in the power of God's love. God is not angry with you. One of the most difficult things for us to believe as Christians is that God is not mad at us. We condemn ourselves because of our past sins or even our present mistakes.

You Are Worthy To Receive a Blessing

The danger in believing that you serve an angry God is that you will begin to feel unworthy of God's goodness or His favor. In turn, you begin to doubt and have fear. Leaving you vulnerable to the enemy's lies. You don't have to *do* something "good" to earn God's love. He will not withhold His love when you do something contrary to His will. It is arrogant for us to believe that we could do anything to "deserve" God's love. We could never *do* anything greater than what Christ did on the Cross; and it is through Christ that we have been made heirs to the promises of God—not through our church attendance, auxiliary service, or what we put in a collection plate.

All of the things that we do should not be in an attempt to "deserve" God's favor, but rather because we love God and are thankful to Him. When we live life trying to deserve the promises, we will fail—miserably. Not only that, we will place ourselves in a position that God never intended for us to be in—as saviors, redeemers, and judges. We try to be so good and do so much that we inadvertently, through works, discount Jesus. We try to save ourselves and redeem ourselves, which is impossible. To make matters worse, we then project this mentality onto others and become judges of one another. If the enemy can get you to believe that God is angry with you or doesn't love you because of something you have done, then he has succeeded in deceiving you into believing that you are not fit to receive God's promises. But you are, because of Jesus. It's not that we deserve it. It's that we are heirs and are entitled to the promises through Christ—by faith.

Our "good" works do not make God love us more. Nor do our "bad" works make Him love us less. This is a deception used by the enemy. He deceives us into believing that God will not be there for us because we have not been "good enough" or that we are experiencing tough times because God no longer loves us.

These are all lies. When we do wrong, we separate ourselves from God's love because we are deceived into believing that we no longer deserve it. Not so. These are all lies. It's difficult sometimes to recognize the lies because the enemy so cleverly mixes the lies in with a few facts. It may be a fact that you haven't found your soul mate, and it may be a fact that you sit home alone. But that does not mean that you are worthless, unwanted, or unloved. Those are lies. God said he will never leave you or forsake you, and that He takes pleasure in giving you the desires of your heart. So if God knows you want a lasting, healthy relationship, He is happy to give you just that. Trust that He is working on your behalf. Let Him perfect you and the other person, and in His timing, it will happen. Just stay faithful.

Christ lives in you—God's love lives in you. That love is there for you no matter what. Just like a parent would never stop loving a child, God will never stop loving you.

Stopping feeling like you don't "deserve" God's love. Through Christ, you *already* have God's love. Receive it. God sees you through the righteousness of His Son Jesus, not through your own righteousness—if there is such a thing! There is no way you can feel God's love that strongly, and want to live in sin. God's love is a light, and that light will not be overshadowed by darkness. Out of a grateful heart we give our lives to Him, and we long for the words of our mouths and the meditations of our hearts to be acceptable in His sight (see Psalm 19:14).

God's unconditional love is not an I-can-do-wrong-and-get-off-scot-free card. When we *truly* receive God's love and it begins to overflow in our hearts, we *will* desire to live a life that pleases God. There is no way you can be enveloped in God's love and want to live in sin. God's love is a light, and that light will not be overshadowed by darkness. Out of a thankful heart, we give our lives to Him, and we long for our words and thoughts and actions to be acceptable to Him. Now that's good news! It's definitely something to be thankful for.

The devil is a liar. He is the father of lies (see John 8:44). Satan is destined to eternal damnation. He is damned, and he wants to take as many lost souls with him as he possibly can. But he can't take you! Don't let the bad things in life make you believe God doesn't love you. God gave us dominion.

> *And God said, Let Us make man in Our image, after Our likeness: and let them have dominion over the fish of the sea, and over the fowl of the air, and over the cattle, and over all the earth, and over every creeping thing that creepeth upon the earth* (Genesis 1:26).

The enemy knows you have dominion and authority, but he is counting on you being weak. He is hoping that you will be easily deceived like Eve was. In Genesis 3:1-7 we get an account of the conversation that Eve had with satan. You'll notice Eve started off on the right foot by countering satan's lies with the words God:

> *And he said unto the woman, Yea, hath God said, Ye shall not eat of every tree of the garden? And the woman said unto the serpent, We may eat of the fruit of the trees of the garden: but of the fruit of the tree which is in the midst of the garden, God hath said, Ye shall not eat of it, neither shall ye touch it, lest ye die* (Genesis 3:1-3).

See what I mean? Eve was doing well. She knew what God said, and she was questioning the enemy's lies and comparing them to God's truth. But then something happened:

> *And the serpent said unto the woman, Ye shall not surely die: for God doth know that in the day ye eat thereof, then your eyes shall be opened, and ye shall be as gods, knowing good and evil. And when the woman saw that the tree was good for food, and that it was pleasant to the eyes, and a tree to be desired to make one wise, she took of the fruit thereof, and did eat, and gave also unto her husband with her* (Genesis 3:4-6).

Eve made the mistake of continuing the communication. When the enemy is shooting negative lies, the last thing you should do is continue to listen to him feed you more lies (meditation). Once you realize the thoughts are false, speak the Word of God and move on. Don't entertain that lie anymore. The devil is a liar, the father of lies. Even when those negative thoughts seem partially true, remember that if they are not what God said then they are lies. Any questions you have, go to God in prayer or seek wise counsel. Satan traps so many of us with half-truths and deceptions. In First Timothy 2:14 it says, "And Adam was not deceived, but the woman being deceived was in the transgression."

We know our debts are out of control, so the enemy tells us, "You're broke; stop giving." Even though we know God says, "While the earth remaineth, seedtime and harvest, and cold and heat, and summer and winter, and day and night shall not cease" (Genesis 8:22). So what happens? Instead of trusting what God says, we start entertaining the negative thoughts from the enemy, that we don't have enough money to pay our bills. We question God's intentions—maybe He didn't mean *always* give. We let the enemy in our head talk us out of what God has promised, and we stop the flow of seedtime to harvest time in our finances. In our hearts, we know God wants us to be givers. Scripture says that God loves a cheerful giver (see 2 Corinthians 9:6-7). Whether you're sowing volunteer time, emotional support, ministry work— whatever you sow, God will multiply and return it to you.

Here are a few examples of the lies you should never believe about God:

- God doesn't love me.

- God is too busy for my problems.

- My problems are too big for God.

- I'm alone. God is not there.

- God can't heal my disease.

- God is going to punish me for my sins.

These are lies, lies, lies—all lies. When we stop giving of ourselves, the enemy laughs because, just like he deceived Eve into eating the fruit and deceived Naomi into depression and changing her name, he has deceived us as well. What lies has he tried to tell you lately? Whatever the lie is, you don't have to be afraid—or live the rest of your life in bondage. God gave you power to break free. It's time for you to unleash it and live victoriously.

God Loves You No Matter What

While we don't encourage sin or even condone it, we do know that the Bible tells us, "There is therefore now no condemnation to them which are in Christ Jesus" (Romans 8:1). I posted a word of encouragement on my Facebook page that I believe applies to this chapter:

Regardless of disagreements among siblings and family, when an outsider threatens a family member, we rise against that attacker to protect them. Though your actions don't always please God, when the enemy threatens to destroy you, God raises a standard against him to protect you. You have protection. Not because you do everything right, but because you are in God's family. Receive it by faith.

You are part of the family of God. He loves you and wants to protect you. Here are some daily confessions based on Romans 8 and Isaiah 54. Meditating on these truths will help you to address your feelings of condemnation and fears of inadequacy because you incorrectly believe that God is angry with you.

- I have an unconditional covenant with God.

- God loves me. He calls me friend.

- God is not angry with me. He loves me.

- The mountains and the hills will pass away before God's covenant promise to love me and give me peace can ever be broken.

- God has sworn never to rebuke me or to be angry with me.

- God's covenant of peace will never leave me.

- God cannot lie to me.

- My righteousness is of the Lord. I am not condemned. I am loved by God.

Make these confessions whenever your heart is tempted with doubt, and know that God loves you regardless of your past, present, or future mistakes. Seek to do good and please Him with your life.

Allow His love to fill your heart and overflow in your life. You do not serve an angry God. Meditate on Isaiah 54:

> *"Though the mountains be shaken and the hills be removed, yet My unfailing love for you will not be shaken nor My covenant of peace be removed," says the Lord, who has compassion on you* (Isaiah 54:10 NIV).

You serve a loving God. Hills will be removed and mountains shaken before God's love will ever be taken away from you or His covenant with you broken. Believe that. Receive it and walk in victory. God is love, and God loves us—with all of our issues and faults. Jehovah is not waiting to condemn you or to punish you. He wants to bless you. He's waiting to help you and heal the hurt. It doesn't matter how much wrong you've done or how many mistakes you've made or will make. He only wants to bless you. He is mindful of you, and no human could ever love you as much as He does! God is your Provider, Peace, and Healer. He wants the best for you, and you have to get into the habit of talking like it.

One thing that will help is meditating on the names of God. Learning who He is will help you understand His character and how much He loves you and wants you to succeed in life.

> *O Lord, our Lord, how excellent is Thy name in all the earth!* (Psalm 8:1)

When you know who God is, you can't help but feel comforted and empowered. Everything that you could possibly need is in the Father. He *is* whatever you need Him to be, and He is waiting for you to come to Him. Whatever you need, God *is!* God told Moses in Exodus, "I Am That I Am" (Exodus 3:14). Don't put limits on God's ability to heal your body or repair your broken heart. God loves you and wants you to be prosperous in every area of your life. Before you allow someone to tell you that God doesn't love you or that He cannot help you, remember the words "I Am That I Am."

He is love, provision, protection, peace, healing, et cetera. The list goes on and on. Let's take a look at some of the most common characteristics of God our Father.

God is your Creator. He loves you. He wants to provide for you. His desire is to heal you and bring you peace in your storms. You are righteous because of His Son Jesus, and He is always with you, even at this moment. There is no need to speak doom and gloom. God has a good plan for your life. The problems you are facing come from the enemy, not the Father (see Jeremiah 29:11). When you know God, you know His nature. By nature, God is love, and that love is unconditional for believers in Jesus Christ.

Let God's perfect love cast away your doubts and fears. Go forth. Call those "things that be not" as though they are (see Romans 4:17). Choose your words carefully from this day forward. Use them to create a life that you enjoy living. Remember:

Meditation + Declaration = Manifestation

Dismiss negative thoughts, words, and feelings. Study your Father's character. Meditate on His Word. Declare it, and watch your life change for the better.

What's in you will come out. The only way that we can consistently speak faith-filled words is if those words are "in us" or abundant in our hearts. "For out of the abundance of the heart the mouth speaketh" (Matthew 12:34). For God's Word to flourish in our hearts, we must sow seeds of the Word through daily prayer, mediation, and study.

The Word of God in our hearts takes root and produces a bumper crop of manifestation and breakthrough—so that when we open our mouth to speak, faith-filled words will overflow from it. Actively seek God's guidance and practice speaking faith-filled words daily. It may feel forced or "fake" at first. You may be tempted to give up, but please don't.

Yes, Jesus Loves You Too

Look to Jesus, the author and finisher of our faith, who for the joy that was set before Him endured the cross, despising the shame, and was set down at the right hand of the throne of God (see Hebrews 12:2). Jesus cares what happens to you. He cares about your dreams and your desires. He totally changed the outcome of Simon Peter and Andrew's day of fishing on the lake of Galilee. He told them where to cast their nets. All they had to do was trust Him enough to follow instructions. Simon answered, "Master, we have toiled all the night, and have taken nothing: nevertheless at Thy word I will let down the net" (Luke 5:5).

Your aspirations matter to God. Don't give up or get discouraged because you seem to be toiling and not getting anywhere. Jesus can change the outcome of your situation with one simple instruction. He knows who you should network with and where your future clients are. Trust Him and let Him effect a positive change in your career or your business aspirations, as only He can.

It would have been enough if He'd stopped there, but He didn't. He took their aspiration and encouraged them to go a step further—to use their knowledge of fishing to bring men and women into the Kingdom of God. You see, it all leads back to the Kingdom. Every God-given skill and desire matters to God, because He wants your joy to be full (see John 16:24), but also because He needs you to help bring others into the family of Christ. When we think of Jesus, we tend to mainly think of Him at His death, burial, and resurrection in the sense that He delivered us from eternal damnation (see John 3:17). We believe that we have eternal life in heaven because of Jesus, but we don't fully believe that we have a right to a healthy, healed, and blessed life on earth. "The Son of God was manifested, that He might destroy the works of the devil" (1 John 3:8).

Sickness and disease, whether physical or mental, are the work of the enemy—your enemy. Jesus, the Word, was made flesh and was born as a man to destroy your sickness and disease. Lay aside every weight. Stay focused. Know that giants do fall. Jesus is the Creator of life, grace, and redemption (see John 20:31; Philippians 4:6-7). Live like you have an inheritance. Jesus left you an inheritance of healing, wealth, peace, and salvation. It's in the Will of God—the Bible. You're entitled to health and healing. "He himself bore our sins in His body on the tree, so that we might die to sin and live to righteousness. By His wounds you have been healed" (1 Peter 2:24 ESV).

Your Sins Have Been Pardoned

During a conversation, someone once suggested that sickness and disease are a form of punishment from God. That is simply not true. Some people are ignorant of this fact.

Consider this—Jesus died for our healing. Why would God do the opposite and make us sick?

Nothing you've done wrong is bigger than what Jesus did on the cross. God wants you well, healthy, prosperous, and full of joy. Don't let ignorant comments plant seeds of doubt, causing you to question whether the God you serve is actually punishing you for something you did wrong. Please be cautious with assigning blame and making assumptions about why someone is experiencing misfortune. Only God knows the whole story.

Just because God didn't stop it from occurring doesn't mean He causes or condones what is happening. Pray that God's love will abound in your heart so that you will know the truth of Jesus's sacrifice.

You Are Forgiven

Bless the Lord, O my soul…who forgiveth all thine iniquities, who healeth all thy diseases (Psalm 103:2-3).

Don't let your past mistakes convince you that you deserve to be sick. Jesus forgives and heals. Once you ask for forgiveness and forgive others, you can, by faith, take hold of your healing with confidence. Find healing verses in Scripture, and meditate on them. Say like Jacob, "I won't let go until You bless me!" (see Genesis 32:26).

You Are Saved

Yes, Jesus died for your salvation. You can't see it, but you believe you are saved. Have the same faith in your healing.

Though you have prayed for it, you may not see it right away, but I urge you to believe you are healed. That's one of the things my aunt and I talked about quite often. I asked her one day, "What would you say if your oncologist told you that you were not saved?"

Without missing a beat she blurted, "He can't tell me I'm not saved."

She was sure of her salvation. She was positive that Jesus had saved her and she was going to heaven. I wanted her to see her healing in the same manner. "Exactly." I leaned forward. "And no doctor can tell you that Jesus hasn't already healed you either."

Jesus took your sickness upon His body on the cross. He suffered for your healing. Receive it by faith. He's ready to forgive you of your sins and heal you of your diseases (see Psalm 103:3).

Salvation is just part of your blessing. If someone gave you a gift, would you cut it in half and give part of it back? Of course not, but we so often only accept half of our inheritance. We receive salvation by faith, but the remainder of our blessing we choose to leave behind. Pray:

> *Father, forgive me for doubting Your Word.*
> *I repent of my sins. I forgive those who have*
> *wronged me, and I believe I am forgiven.*
> *Thank You for Your mercy, grace, and*
> *comforting Spirit. I receive my healing right*
> *now through the mighty name of Jesus.*
> *By His stripes I was healed and I am now*
> *made whole, in Jesus's name, amen.*

Be Steadfast and Unmovable

Cast your cares on Him—He cares for you (see 1 Peter 5:7). Turn your focus toward healing. Be steadfast and unmovable in your faith. When you trust in someone, you feel secure, calm, and reassured. That's how we should feel about the Word of God—secure, calm, and reassured.

> *Blessed assurance, Jesus is mine! Oh, what a foretaste of glory divine! Heir of salvation, purchase of God, born of His Spirit, washed in His blood.*
> —FANNY J. CROSBY, "Blessed Assurance"

Be assured that His healing power is as much for you today as it was for the woman with the issue of blood (see Matthew 9), the lame man at the gate called Beautiful (see Acts 3), the man with the withered hand (see Mark 3), or Peter's mother-in-law, sick with fever (see Matthew 8).

Be hopeful and positive. Hope is seeing something that isn't there. It's seeing yourself healthy and whole. Give thanks to God—not for the illness, but for the grace to overcome and for God's goodness to perform a great work in your life.

Don't look in the mirror on your wall. Look in the mirror of God's grace. See yourself healthy and doing the things you love, spending time with the people you love. Romans 5:20 says, "Where sin abounded, grace did much more abound." I believe that where sickness abounds, grace will much more abound!

FAITH DECLARATION

The joy of the Lord strengthens me.
I am humble before the Lord.

He is lifting me up! The Lord has
set me high above my enemy.

He has commanded His angels to help me.

God's grace is greater than anything I face.

Nothing is happening without His permission.

No matter what, I trust Him.

God is watching over me.

DISCUSSION QUESTIONS

1. Why do you think some find it difficult to believe God loves them unconditionally?

2. How much does God love you? How do you know?

3. Describe a time in your life when you experienced or felt the presence of God's love.

4. How can we help the rest of the world to understand God's love?

5. What way does God's love influence your self-esteem?

6. Jesus loved us so much that He sacrificed His own life. Have you ever made a sacrifice for someone because you loved them? Was the experience good or bad? What happened?

Chapter 12

DISCERNING THE VOICES

We need discernment in what we see and
what we hear and what we believe.
—CHARLES R. SWINDOLL

If you are to overcome negative self-talk, it's crucial that you are able to discern the voices in your head. You have to be able to judge the voices and know the difference between voices of light and voices of darkness. God is love, and as such His voice is one of love. It's your belief in the power of His love that will open your spiritual ears so that you can recognize His voice when you hear it. Studies show that a fetus begins to recognize his mother's voice around 32 to 34 weeks. I believe that. During both my pregnancies I made it a point to read and talk to my unborn sons daily—not just so they could hear my voice, but so they would recognize it. I wanted them to hear the love in my voice and to recognize the voice of love that would support and encourage them for the rest of their lives.

The Stranger's Voice

The phrase *stranger danger* is most notably associated with child safety. It's a phrase used to remind children that it's dangerous to trust people they do not know—people who are up to no good who will do them harm. As believers we must be aware of the enemy's voice. We must understand the danger of trusting the stranger's voice. The stranger is the enemy. Going back to Jesus's response to the religious leaders, He said, "A stranger will [my sheep] not follow, but will flee from him: for they know not the voice of strangers" (John 10:5).

When we get caught up in life's drama, stress, and chaos, we may be tempted to listen to the voice of the stranger—the voice that's telling you give up, end it all, there's no way out. The stranger's voice is up to no good. It means to harm you and lead you astray. In Peter's case, the voice of doubt caused him to sink.

The Stranger's Voice Tells You You're Sinking

Seeing Jesus walk on water motivated Peter to do the extraordinary. Something inside him knew, with the help of Jesus, he could do what seemed impossible to the others who were seeing the same miracle. Without hesitation he asked, "Lord, if it be thou, bid me come" (Matthew 14:28). Peter just needed to hear Jesus say the words. He just needed to hear the Shepherd's voice. All you need is a word from the Lord, and you can accomplish what seems impossible to everyone else. But it's going to take faith that you can do something that no one else in your family has done, that everyone else is afraid to do. The encouraging voice of Jesus bidding you to come will give you the courage to walk on water.

I can imagine after taking the first couple of steps Peter must have thought, "Wow! I can walk on water!" But then something happened and Peter began to sink. What was it that caused him to lose the confidence that he'd had just moments earlier?

Peter stopped listening to the voice that told him to come forth. Instead, he started listening to the stranger in his head saying, "This is impossible. You're going to die! Look at all this water."

How often do we do just what Peter did? How often do we stop listening to the voice of God and fixate on what's happening around us instead? We start hearing, "I don't have as much education as they do. My business is going to fail. I don't know what's ahead."

Sinking is a state of mind caused by focusing on all the wrong things. Fix your eyes on the Father. He knows the plans He has for us—plans to prosper us and not harm us. Plans to give us hope and a future (see Jeremiah 29:11).

The Stranger's Voice Tries to Talk You Out of Your Destiny

In Matthew 16, Jesus asked the disciples, "Who do you say I am?" It was Peter who enthusiastically said, "You are the Messiah, Son of the living God" (see Matthew 16:15-16). Peter's response showed that he had a deep and intimate understanding of Jesus's power and purpose. Because of that, Jesus praised him: "Blessed art thou, Simon Barjona: for flesh and blood hath not revealed it unto thee, but My Father which is in heaven" (Matthew 16:17). Peter was already thinking on a heavenly level. He was operating on the knowledge that there was a world more powerful and meaningful than the one he was living in.

If God says He plans to give us a future, why are we focusing on the pain of the past or the pressures of the present? Our eyes have to be focused on the bright future God has promised. That why Scripture says, "Jesus...for the joy that was set before him endured the cross, despising the shame" (Hebrews 12:2).

Like Peter, we sometimes take our focus off the promises and principles of God and begin to sink. Or we start out successful with great confidence, but then we get derailed by tough economic times or things that don't work out the way we thought they should. We get focused on our limitations, and all of a sudden we're sinking. Where we were once full of confidence and enthusiasm, we are suddenly fearful and timid.

The Stranger's Voice Tries to Convince You That Slavery Is Good

The children of Israel had a burst of confidence when they were liberated from slavery. They were excited and rejoiced at the opportunity to live as free men and women in a new land overflowing with milk and honey. But each time they experienced a challenge, they wanted to quit. Some even want to return to Egypt. The slavery that they'd come from seemed better in their eyes than walking into the unknown.

They were not focused on the promise that God made them; they were focused on the conditions around them. "Milk and honey" was just days away, but because they complained and doubted God so much, He allowed them to wander for forty years, many of them dying without ever getting a glimpse of the Promised Land.

The enemy will always encourage you to stay the same. He doesn't want you to grow spiritually, financially, emotionally, or otherwise. So he magnifies the obstacles and hardships in your way to make you second-guess your goals and dreams. To make you think, "Maybe I should just go back to Egypt." Paul wrote these words to the church at Corinth: "You say, 'I am allowed to do anything'—but not everything is good for you. And even though 'I am allowed to do anything,' I must not become a slave to anything" (1 Corinthians 6:12 NLT).

Don't believe the lie that doing what you want, when you want, with whomever you want is freedom. It's not. If it causes harm to you or others, it's ungodly; if you're addicted to it, then you are in slavery. The good news is God is ready and willing to set you free, and whoever the Son sets free is free indeed (see John 8:36)!

Don't let the negative voices convince you to turn back to drugs, sex, gambling, negativity, fear. The adversity you face is nothing compared to God's power. God is faithful to deliver you. Stay focused on the Promised Land. Look to Jesus, the author and finisher of our faith, who for the joy that was set before him endured the cross, despising the shame, and was set down at the right hand of the throne of God.

The Stranger's Voice Will Tempt You

And when the tempter came to Him, he said, If thou be the Son of God, command that these stones be made bread. But He answered and said, It is written, Man shall not live by bread alone, but by every word that proceedeth out of the mouth of God (Matthew 4:3-4).

If the enemy had the audacity to try and tempt Jesus, surely we must know that he will try to tempt us as well. That voice that is telling you to follow your flesh is the voice of the enemy. He does not love you. He could not care less about you living holy or trying to please God. He only wants you to get caught in the web of lies, deception, and lust. The tempter's voice tells you to do what makes you feel good.

This voice never tells you of the consequences. It never warns that addictions, fornication, cheating, and lying all lead to destruction. That you could destroy yourself and others in the process. Don't confuse this voice with God's. James 1:13 says, "Let no man say when he is tempted, I am tempted of God: for God cannot be tempted with evil, neither tempteth He any man." God will never pressure you to do something evil or wrong. He won't put you in a compromising relationship, nor will He send people into your life who influence you to do wrong. Pray about these things. Discern the voice. It's not God. It's the enemy. Read First Peter 2:11 for exhortation. "Dearly beloved, I beseech you as strangers and pilgrims, abstain from fleshly lusts, which war against the soul."

Remember the formula:

Meditation + Declaration = Manifestation.

The negative thoughts you meditate on will manifest. The evil thoughts tempting you must be cast down with the Word. If you think about them too long, those evil thoughts will become sinful manifestations, like they did for Ananias and his wife, Sapphira, in Acts 5. The enemy tempted them to lie to God. They gave in to the temptation and ultimately paid the price of sin with their lives.

Silencing the Stranger's Voice

The greatest examples we have of how to silence the enemy's voice come from our Lord and Savior, Jesus Christ. Atop Mount Hermon, He said, "Get thee behind me, Satan." In response to Satan's temptations, He boldly countered, "It is written." And in the garden of Gethsemane, after praying until sweat poured as drops of blood, He said, "Not my will but thine be done."

Get Thee Behind Me, Satan!

As Jesus and His disciples stood atop Mount Hermon, He explained to them that he was to be arrested, tortured, and crucified. Peter took Jesus aside and rebuked Him, saying, "Never, Lord! This shall never happen to you!" In Peter's mind this was the right thing to say. But look at how Jesus responded: "Get behind Me, satan! You are a stumbling block to Me; you do not have in mind the concerns of God, but merely human concerns" (Matthew 16:22-23 NIV).

When the voices of negativity speak, you have authority to say, "Get behind me!" Maybe someone is speaking negativity into your ear or telling you to give up. Don't let the enemy deceive you. Recognize that they are being used as a stumbling block and they may not even realize it. Their words are not those of God, but of "human concerns." If you are believing God, these words are not what you need to hear. The enemy is using ignorance to discourage you. Rebuke the enemy and stay in faith.

You have to spiritually discern what is coming from God and what is being used by the enemy to discourage you, or it will damage your thinking about your situation and make you begin to wonder, "Maybe God won't heal this for me." Like my aunt, maybe you hear so many bad statistics that you replay the words over and over in your mind until worry and stress weaken you and steal your faith. Recognize these mental attacks for what they are—a ploy of the enemy to steal, kill, and destroy your faith.

The devil is a liar. James 4:7 tells us, "Submit yourselves therefore to God. Resist the devil, and he will flee from you." To submit means to put yourself under God's authority. Whatever the problem you're facing, submit it to the authority of the Almighty, and use the Word of God as your weapon to stand against the enemy and silence his voice.

It Is Written

After forty days and nights of fasting food and drink, Jesus, in His humanity, was physically and mentally vulnerable. That's when the devil struck. He tried to tempt Jesus at

His weakest point. Satan is still using this same tactic today. When we're at our lowest point, he slithers in and attempts to capitalize on our insecurities, fears, and weaknesses.

> *And after fasting forty days and forty nights, He was hungry. And the tempter came and said to Him, "If you are the Son of God, command these stones to become loaves of bread." But He answered, "It is written, 'Man shall not live by bread alone, but by every word that comes from the mouth of God'"* (Matthew 4:2-4 ESV).

All of those months that I was communicating back and forth with the bank, wondering if I was going to lose my home, I struggled to stay in faith. When the enemy tried to tell me that my home was going into foreclosure, I cast those thoughts down and thanked God that my home was delivered. I started that modification process in June. The days turned to months. I became emotionally exhausted. I was tempted to give up. But I stayed the course of faith and daily I confessed, "A thousand homes may foreclose by my side, ten thousand by my right hand, but no foreclosure shall come near my home" (see Psalm 91:7). It wasn't until January of the following year that I finally received approval for my loan modification and my home was delivered. God is faithful. That may sound like no big deal to you, but it was a difficult time for me as a single mom and struggling entrepreneur. Perhaps you are facing something way more serious. I encourage you to trust and believe Him with all your heart.

Speak the Word in the presence of temptation, just as Jesus did. When the bills are ninety days past due and there is no money in the bank, don't be tempted to do something illegal or immoral for money. Instead, trust God to send help or open a door of opportunity. Cast down the negative thoughts. Resist the stranger's voice. Know that God can and will help you. Don't be afraid to counter the enemy's tempting words by declaring, "It is written."

Not My Will But Thine Be Done

Jesus knew the terrible fate that awaited Him. He was fully aware that He was going to be ridiculed, horribly beaten, and crucified. It's no wonder He prayed, "Father, if You are willing, take this cup from Me; yet not My will, but Yours be done" (Luke 22:42 NIV).

No challenge we face on earth can compare to what Jesus endured at Calvary, but there are times when we face terrible circumstances. Death, divorce, impairments, life-threatening diseases, a lost child—the list goes on. Though we try to be strong, fear grips us so tightly that we pray and hope for God to intervene and save us from the situation so that we don't have to endure the pain, hurt, or humiliation.

Years ago, I remember a time when I cried myself to sleep every night. I didn't want to call my family because they'd warned me about the relationship that I was in, and I didn't want to hear "I told you so." As the tears streamed, I begged God to help me find a way out. I didn't want to go through the pain anymore. I felt rejected and humiliated. My heart literally ached from all of the pain and disappointment.

The thought of staying in that situation for one more day, week, or month was more than I thought I could bear. I didn't think I would make it through—but I did. At a time when I had no one else, God was present. I trusted Him. I took my eyes off the problem and started looking for answers in the Word. I prayed, "Not my will." I changed. I stopped walking around looking sad. I made a choice to go through the valley—not live there. I wish I could say the relationship was salvaged, but it wasn't. But even though the relationship ended, my life didn't. There is life after death. There's a new beginning after death, divorce, job loss, dysfunction, pain; and, as Jesus showed us, there's a better life even after you've been crucified.

Let God have His way in your life. Just because life has placed you in a terrible situation, that doesn't mean you're defeated. Go to God in prayer with the attitude that His will is your desire. If your situation is a result of a poor choice, don't condemn yourself. There will be plenty of people lined up to do that for you. God is not holding anything against you. Silence the stranger's voice once and for all. Declare, "Not my will Lord, but Thine be done!"

The Shepherd's Voice

In John 10, when the religious leaders asked Jesus, "Are you the Messiah?" Jesus responded, "I did tell you, but you do not believe. The works I do in My Father's name testify about Me, but you do not believe because you are not My sheep. My sheep listen to My voice; I know them, and they follow Me" (John 10:25-27).

As followers of Christ, we listen with our hearts. We hear Jesus. We recognize His voice, and we listen to it. It is the voice of life more abundantly. We know that the Shepherd would never lead us astray. His words are comforting and reassuring. His words build you up and encourage you to be your best self.

Jesus lives in you. He knows you inside and out. You are created in the image of His Father. God created you. He knows you. His voice is the only voice that you should allow to speak into your heart. His words are the only words that you should speak over your life and the lives of others.

When the chatter in your head begins, discern the voices. Is it the voice of a God who knows and loves you? Or is it the voice of a stranger who means you no good? Why listen to someone who doesn't know you? Why listen to anyone other than your creator?

Jesus also said, "My Father, which gave them Me, is greater than all; and no man is able to pluck them out of My Father's hand" (John 10:29). When we have an intimate relationship with the Shepherd, we will not be fooled by the stranger. We will flee from the stranger's voice. We won't listen to his lies. We will be assured that our worth is in Christ, our success is in the Savior, and we won't allow our self-worth to be snatched away by negative self-talk. We recognize the danger of the stranger's voice, and we seek the voice of the Shepherd for guidance.

The Shepherd's Voice Will Validate You

Thoughts and feelings of hopelessness and failure had been tormenting me all day. I had such a spirit of heaviness that day. After moping around the house for most of the day, I finally shuffled into my bedroom and fell to my knees. For the next fifteen minutes or so, I talked to God about everything that was bothering me, from my writing aspirations and financial goals to my children and their future.

I wish that I could say I felt better immediately afterward, but I didn't. I continued on with my day, only now I had become like an overanxious toddler, waiting impatiently for God to give me some sort of an encouraging word. It wasn't until late that evening (our impatience doesn't make God move any faster) that God encouraged my spirit with these words: "Your life matters to me."

That simple phrase made me think about John 3:16: "For God so loved the world, that He gave His only begotten Son, that whosoever believeth in Him should not perish, but have everlasting life." No matter what I've done, how many shortcomings I have, or how many times I've second-guessed Him, He still loves me. My life matters, and God proved that love by sending His Son, Jesus. His effect on our lives has been profound and miraculous.

Your life matters. The world is a better place with you in it. If it matters to you, it matters to God. Your dreams are not frivolous or stupid. Jesus cares what happens to you. He cares about your dreams and your desires.

The Shepherd's Voice Will Comfort You

Who comforteth us in all our tribulation, that we may be able to comfort them which are in any trouble, by the comfort wherewith we ourselves are comforted of God (2 Corinthians 1:4).

I learned a long time ago that loneliness has nothing to do with whether or not there are people around you. No matter who you are or what you are going through at this moment, let me make one thing very clear. The Lord is with you. He is there to comfort you, but you have to let Him.

You have to shut out all of the other voices that are telling you that you're worthless. Pay no attention to the stranger. His goal is to lead you astray. Listening to the negative voices will only make your journey through the valley longer than it needs to be.

The help you need is not in a prescription bottle. It's in Jesus. Cast your cares on the Lord; you matter to Him. He cares what you're going through. It's the Shepherd's voice that will lead you through and comfort you in the midst of the trials and tribulations of life.

The Shepherd's Voice Will Calm Your Storm

In Luke 8 the tumultuous waves and raging winds were so fierce that it seemed almost certain that the ship and crew would be destroyed. Filled with terror, the disciples ran to find Jesus who, to their surprise, was soundly sleeping in the lower part of the vessel.

When Jesus woke up, He went onto the upper part of the ship, spoke to the winds, and commanded, "Peace, be still." The wind and the waves obeyed His command. After everything settled, He turned to the disciples and asked, "Where is your faith?" Though they should not have been afraid of dying, especially with Jesus on board, they allowed fear to grip them when the storm arose. They lost faith.

For some people a storm could be the sudden death of a loved one or an unexpected diagnosis of a disease. For others the storm will be a prodigal child or seemingly irreparably damaged relationship. When the challenge (storm) comes, it may fill your head with doubt and fear. You may even fear that you will drown as your life takes a beating from the fierce winds of pain and the pounding of stress. The storm may shake the very core of your being and make you wonder if Jesus is on board or even cares.

As we pass from one season of life to another, storms may arise that will cause our faith to be shaken. But we should not be afraid, because we have Jesus in our lives. Stand boldly in the time of trouble, rebuke the winds that threaten to destroy you, and declare peace in the name of Jesus. Jesus is on board and He does care.

He lives in you and "greater is He that is in you" than any challenge you face in this world (see 1 John 4:4). By faith, we can and will overcome every struggle and adversity. But we first have to know and believe, trusting God and having faith, knowing He will not allow the circumstances to destroy us. Not everyone's storm is the same, but our Lord is the same. It doesn't matter what the storm is. What matters is that you maintain faith in the power of the Lord's presence. No matter how bad the storms in your life become, He has the authority over the wind and waves. He can calm every storm by simply speaking, "Peace, be still." Remember that the next time you are going through a difficult time. If the voices in your head are saying something contrary to "Peace, be still," it's not the voice of the Shepherd. I'll end this chapter with the words of a poem:

When storms arise
And dark'ning skies
About me threat'ning lower,
To Thee, O Lord, I raise mine eyes,
To Thee my tortured spirit flies
For solace in that hour.

The mighty arm
Will let no harm
Come near me nor befall me;
Thy voice shall quiet my alarm,
When life's great battle waxeth warm—
No foeman shall appall me.

Upon Thy breast
Secure I rest,
From sorrow and vexation;
No more by sinful cares oppressed,
But in Thy presence ever blest,
O God of my salvation.

—"Hymn," PAUL LAURENCE DUNBAR

FAITH DECLARATION

I am spiritually dressed for success.

The belt of truth is firmly fastened.

*The breastplate of His righteousness
protects my chest.*

*My feet are firmly planted in
the Gospel of peace.*

The helmet of salvation crowns my head.

*My shield of faith is lifted, and I have a
firm hold on the sword of the Spirit.*

DISCUSSION QUESTIONS

1. How can you recognize the Shepherd's voice? What are the characteristics?

2. How do you silence the stranger's voice? What are the characteristics?

3. Why is it so important to discern between the two voices?

4. How can you tell the difference between the enemy's lies and God's truth?

5. Have you ever been in a situation where you took your eyes off God and started focusing on your problem? What happened? What did you learn from that experience?

Chapter 13

DEVELOPING YOUR SPIRITUAL SELF-TALK

If this inner and critical voice has kept you safe for many years as your inner voice of authority, you may end up not being able to hear the real voice of God.
—RICHARD ROHR

By now you understand that one of the most powerful tools God has given you is the ability to speak life. In this chapter I will show you how to create life-giving declarations that will inspire you, build your faith, and help you create the life God intended for you to experience on earth.

Some of the most famous, successful, and well-known people in the world use daily affirmations as part of their daily routines to help them achieve focus, clarity, and peace of mind. When creating and using spiritual self-talk, you must keep in mind the three essential areas we discussed in the previous chapter—your heart, your mind, and the words of your mouth. God is more concerned with the condition of your heart. You can recite, memorize, and pontificate Scripture until you're out of breath, but if your heart is clogged with mischief, you can expect nothing to manifest.

Pray for guidance and, if necessary, ask for forgiveness. Then forgive those who have hurt you. Release yourself from the pain of past hurts. Renew your mind. Walk the talk. Talk the walk. These practices combined with daily speaking scriptural affirmations will yield supernatural results in your life. This is Scripture-based self-talk.

"I Am" Self-Talk

When you utilize "I Am" self-talk, you state your desire in a positive way, leaving out negative words or connotations. Instead of focusing on what is wrong, focus on how you want things to be. If you are having health challenges, declare, "I am healed," as opposed to "I'm not sick."

Leaving out the negative words helps you focus more on the positive and leaves out any words or phrases that may introduce doubt or fear. Do focus on the promise you want to manifest, not the problem the enemy has presented before you. Use your "I Am" voice to speak only what is positive.

Positive Outlook Self-Talk

Use Scripture to develop phrases that improve your outlook or how you perceive a difficult situation. One day I stared into my refrigerator; I complained, "I don't have any food." Then I closed the refrigerator, went to the pantry, and took out some flour and other ingredients to bake homemade biscuits. While I was mixing the ingredients, I thought about my words earlier: "I don't have any food."

Here I was with all the ingredients necessary to prepare a meal, yet I was whining that I didn't have any food. As I cut out the biscuits and laid them on the baking sheet, I began to thank God for what I had. My perception changed. Instead of complaining about what I didn't have, I adopted an attitude of gratitude for what I did have.

Sometimes, because we are so busy missing the steak, we forget to thank God for the loaf of bread. We don't have what we want, so we convince ourselves that we don't have anything at all.

The enemy likes to magnify problems. Reciting Scripture-based phrases will help you stay centered on the Word of God. To do this, write down a handful of your favorite scriptures—the ones that encourage you the most. Study and meditate on each of those scriptures. Find out what they mean. Then take a moment to paraphrase each of them in your own voice.

If you need financial provision, based on Ephesians 3:20, say, "I have more than enough to meet my needs." Don't feel like you have to use *thus* and *thou*. If those aren't words you use, they won't sound natural to you and you may be tempted to ignore what you are saying. Instead, use phrases that sound like something you would say.

For example, Second Corinthians 4:17 is one of my favorite scriptures: "Our light affliction, which is but for a moment, worketh for us a far more exceeding and eternal weight of glory." If I were creating an affirmation using

Second Corinthians 4:17, it would sound something like this: "This is just a temporary problem, and it is small compared to the awesome glory I'm going to experience!"

The takeaway here is to remember you don't have to use the exact words used in Scripture. You can use synonyms that don't change the meaning of the verse. You're not rewriting Scripture; you are applying it to your life in a way that is relatable.

Don't fall prey to your self-talk, which may be telling you that you don't have enough. Take a look around you. What do you have? Family, shelter, clothing, ingredients for biscuits? Whatever you have, be grateful. Thank God for it.

"It's Already Done" Self-Talk

Use Scripture-based affirmations that declare as if what you desire has already manifested—by faith declaring, "It's already done!" Take the focus off what you have not accomplished. Stop complaining about what you could have, should have, or would have done. Change your self-talk to reflect God's promise as though you already possessed it. Call those "things that be not" as though they were. Put your faith into action by acting the way you would if your blessing was in your hand.

If God manifested your blessing today, how would you feel? What would you do? Would you be smiling, laughing, and feeling good? I know I would. Go ahead and challenge yourself to act, think, feel, and believe with every fiber of your being that your blessing is present and available. Remember what I said in the introduction about the difference between faithing it verses faking it? That's what you're doing. You are faithing it. You're walking by faith until you see it. Don't allow anyone to discourage you.

FAITH DECLARATION

I only believe what God says about me.

*I embrace the person God created me
to be. I am a magnificent creature.*

I don't need a mirror to tell me I am beautiful.

*God says I am fearfully and
wonderfully made.*

*I declare I am healthy, and I am
whole in mind, body, and spirit.*

*This is His house, and His
craftsmanship is flawless.*

DISCUSSION QUESTIONS

1. How can you use Scripture to create positive self-talk declarations?

2. After reading this chapter, did you realize that you were already using a particular type of self-talk? If so, which one? ("I Am," "Positive Outlook," "It's Already Done"?) If not, which are you more comfortable with or likely to use?

3. Which type of self-talk seems to be the most difficult to implement? Explain.

4. How would you respond to someone who called you a liar or accused you of "faking it"?

5. How many people do you know who speak faith-filled words on a regular basis?

Chapter 14

GOD HAS GIVEN YOU POWER: USE IT

*God, our Creator, has stored within our minds and
personalities great potential strength and ability.
Prayer helps us tap and develop these powers.*
—A. P. J. ABDUL KALAM

God has entrusted much power to His children. Even after
Eve fell victim to the enemy's deceptions, God made her a
promise: "Your seed will bruise his head." He gave her assurance and hope that, while her mistake was severe and carried
a consequence, He still loved her and had her back. The power
He gave her was paramount to the survival of the human race.
She now had the power of a promise that her seed would ultimately destroy the works of the enemy. That seed was Jesus!
"For this purpose the Son of God was manifested, that He
might destroy the works of the devil" (1 John 3:8). It is through
the Savior that we have a relationship with God that cannot be
severed. Nothing can separate us from the love of God. Our

God is almighty and all-powerful, and He has given us, His children, much power. We, the decedents of Eve, continue to birth kings, queens, pastors, bishops, and all manner of leaders into the world. We carry the power of the promise to bruise the enemy's head. We, by the power of the Holy Spirit, bear witness to the Gospel and lead the unsaved to Christ. Heaven rejoices when one sinner repents and joins the family of Christ (see Luke 15:7).

Read Second Corinthians 4:7: "We now have this light shining in our hearts, but we ourselves are like fragile clay jars containing this great treasure" (NLT). This makes it clear that our great power is from God, and not ourselves. Our God who loves us so much has given us great ability, authority, influence, and control.

You don't ever have to fear that this power will run out. God is the Source and He is infinite.

> So he said to me, "This is the Word of the Lord to Zerubbabel: 'Not by might nor by power, but by My Spirit,' says the Lord Almighty" (Zechariah 4:6 NIV).

You're Not a Failure

After my divorce, I felt like a complete failure. I felt weak and powerless. My son had to leave his friends and move to a new school. I had to move back home with my dad. People were gossiping, and worst of all I thought I failed God by getting a divorce. Maybe if I had been a better wife or maybe if I were more attractive. Maybe if I didn't nag, he would have stayed home more. I beat myself up with maybes and what-ifs. I did what satan wanted me to do—sit around crying, complaining, and calling myself a failure.

I was so afraid of failing at marriage that I vowed never to get married again. How silly is that? Marriage is absolutely wonderful, and there are millions of happy couples to prove it. You just don't hear about the happy marriages, because the enemy doesn't want you to. Think about it. You only hear about the ones that fail. People and things fail. Just because you fail does not mean you are a failure. Why would Satan tell you that you are a failure? To break you. To make you talk yourself out of experiencing God's perfect will. To make you so afraid of failing that you never try again. The enemy knows each time you try your chances of succeeding increase. He doesn't want you to succeed. He wants you to break. The truth is: God wants you blessed, filled with self-confidence, and empowered by the power that works in you—His power.

Understand the Power You Possess

To release the power within, you must first recognize that you are not working through your own might. It is the Lord's doing. Isaiah 40:29 says, "He gives strength to the weary and increases the power of the weak" (NIV). If you ever find yourself feeling beat down, like you can't go on, remember this scripture. It is God who gives power to the weak. He will give you power to stand strong again. Trust in the Lord and let Him lead you.

Embrace these powers that He has blessed you with. Know what power you have. Everyone has been given a measure of faith. We all have different skills and talents, but these powers are universal. You can't release what you don't know you possess. Fret not. I'm going to share with you some of the awesome authority that God has given you.

Take the authority you've been given. Don't live life afraid that something is going to defeat you. Don't just endure life, enjoy it. When we read Second Corinthians 3:5, it reminds us that we are not sufficient in ourselves. Our sufficiency comes from God. That's the good news. You don't have to rely on your own ability. It's in God that we move and have our being (see Acts 17:28), and He is unbreakable! When you are rooted in the Word, you know that nothing can separate you from His love. His love covers a multitude of sins, and nothing that comes against you can ever prevail against the love of God. It's too powerful.

#1 *The Power of Prayer*

God hears and answers your prayers. "I call on You, my God, for You will answer me" (Psalm 17:6 NIV). Prayer is our direct communication with God. In the world they say, "It's not what you know but who you know." When you have connections with the right people, you can get things done. You can excel and go further—but I encourage you not to depend on human beings.

Don't get frustrated trying to network your way to the top. You already know the man at the top. You know El Shaddai. Hallelujah! You have the ear of the Almighty God. When you call Him, He will answer you. He can get things done. He can move obstacles and open closed doors. He can give you the power to increase, excel, and go further in life than any boss, executive, president, king, or queen. You don't have to wait in line. He's always available. You don't need an open-door policy or an appointment. You don't have to be in a closet or a special room.

Anytime, anywhere, you can call on Him. Standing in the elevator or in the line at the grocery store. Whispering, crying, or boldly proclaiming, you have the power of prayer. About your kids, your spouse, your job, your self-image—go to Him in prayer. Unleash the power of prayer that is inside you. In His timing, He will answer. In His way, He will provide.

#2 *The Power of Love*

We love others because God first loved us (see 1 John 4:19). When we are emotionally and spiritually healthy, we can love with our whole being. I believe God infused us with His own loving characteristics—nurturing, compassion, loyalty, and protectiveness—all of the qualities that we need to be great sisters, wives, mothers, grandmothers, nieces, aunts, and ministers.

> The way of peace is the way of love. Love is the greatest power on earth. It conquers all things.
> —PEACE PILGRIM

We love one another and our God in a way that only a believer can. Don't be afraid to let the love of God shine in your life. It's that love that will cause sinners to be drawn to you and ultimately to our Lord and Savior, Jesus Christ.

#3 The Power to Get Wealth

> *But remember the Lord your God, for it is He who gives you the ability to produce wealth, and so confirms His covenant, which he swore to your ancestors, as it is today* (Deuteronomy 8:18 NIV).

God does not promise to help us win the lottery or a sweepstakes, but He does promise to bless the works of our hands: "The Lord will open the heavens, the storehouse of His bounty, to send rain on your land in season and to bless all the work of your hands. You will lend to many nations but will borrow from none" (Deuteronomy 28:12 NIV).

Whatever financial goal you are trying to reach, you can do it with God's anointing and favor. But you have to give Him something to work with. It's not realistic to expect Him to increase you unless you are working on something. Nor is it realistic to expect increase if your sole purpose is to hoard it up for yourself and not be a blessing to others.

He cares about your desires. Your goals and dreams matter to Him. Matthew 7:11 says, "If ye then, being evil, know how to give good gifts unto your children, how much more shall your Father which is in heaven give good things to them that ask Him?" As long your financial desires are in keeping with His Word, don't limit God and don't limit yourself. He is ready and waiting for you to unleash the power to get wealth by faith.

#4 *The Power to Speak Life*

> *Death and life are in the power of the tongue: and they that love it shall eat the fruit thereof* (Proverbs 18:21).

This power is what this book is all about. We have the power to call those "things that be not" as though they were (see Romans 4:17). The Word of God spoken from our mouths by faith has power to create favor, blessings, healing, and deliverance. It's not "name it and claim it." It's walking by faith. It's believing that something exists beyond what you see in front of your face. It's declaring what you desire, and your believing God has the power to deliver.

> *Truly I tell you, if anyone says to this mountain, "Go, throw yourself into the sea," and does not doubt in their heart but believes that what they say will happen, it will be done for them* (Mark 11:23 NIV).

#5 *The Power of Courage and Authority*

> *But you will receive power when the Holy Spirit comes upon you. And you will be My witnesses, telling people about Me everywhere* (Acts 1:8 NLT).

The conversation in your head may be: "You can't do it. You're inadequate. Who do you think you are?" But the Lord has commanded the Holy Spirit to come upon you, and when you receive the Holy Spirit, you are endowed with the power of confidence, courage, and supernatural ability.

Child of God, there is work for us to do in the Kingdom. It starts with healing in our own lives and extends to our families, communities, and beyond. It's time to show the world that God has empowered us to achieve awesome works by His Spirit.

#6 *The Power of Forgiveness*

> *And because you belong to Him, the power of the life-giving Spirit has freed you from the power of sin that leads to death* (Romans 8:2 NLT).

If you are born again, you have been set free from sin. Hallelujah! Whatever you did in your past is not being held over your head. Christ says you are not guilty! You are a new creature. You are not condemned. You are forgiven. The power of the Holy Spirit lives inside you, and you have reserved strength for times of weakness. With this power you are capable, confident, and courageous.

Live life free from your past, and invite the Holy Spirit to help you with every challenge you face. "There is therefore now no condemnation to them which are in Christ Jesus, who walk not after the flesh, but after the Spirit" (Romans 8:1).

God is not angry with you, nor is He holding your past against you. You are forgiven. Forgive yourself. and hold your head up high. Then take the mercy you've received and pay it forward. Forgive the people in your life who have wronged you. You have the power to forgive.

Stay connected to the Father so that there is a continual flow of grace, mercy, and love. Studying and mediating on

His Word will keep you plugged in to the ultimate power source. The Lord told us in John 15:4 that if we abide in Him, He will abide in us, and we can ask what we wish and it will be done for us. Abiding in Him is the only way that we have access to living fruitful and productive lives.

God has given us the power to gain victory over depression, divorce, addictions, oppression, sickness, disease, and heartbreak.

> *For the Spirit God gave us does not make us timid, but gives us power, love, and self-discipline* (2 Timothy 1:7 NIV).

The world is in desperate need. Our children are dying. Homes are falling apart. Souls need to be saved, and we have the power within us to make a difference. Our presence as powerful people of God must be felt. It's time to unleash our power.

The rest of this book is composed of daily meditations and Scripture. During your study time, meditate on them and pray for understanding. Ask the Holy Spirit to reveal the value and meaning to you for your life and to show you the areas you need to strengthen.

> *Ask, and it shall be given you; seek, and ye shall find; knock, and it shall be opened unto you* (Matthew 7:7).

FAITH DECLARATION

*Today I am thankful. I have a
grateful heart, and I am content.*

I am at peace, and forgiveness floods my heart.

*I only desire what God has for me,
and I am open to receive it.*

God's favor abounds toward me.

*I patiently await the magnificent
manifestation of God's blessings to
come upon me and overtake me.*

Any day now I will reap if I faint not.

DISCUSSION QUESTIONS

1. Of the six powers mentioned (prayer, getting wealth, speaking life, forgiveness, courage, and authority) which power resonates with you the most? Why?

2. Is there one power mentioned that you would like to learn more about? Why is it important to you?

3. How do we as believers receive power?

4. Do we have the same power that God has? Explain your answer.

5. Why is it so important for believers to understand the power of God that works through them?

6. What can we do to make sure that God receives the glory for the work He does in our lives, and not us?

DAILY REFLECTIONS
AND
MEDITATIONS

Day 1

YOUR WORDS CAN KILL

Scripture Reading

Death and life are in the power of the tongue: and they that love it shall eat the fruit thereof (Proverbs 18:21).

Today's Meditation

Your words can kill or give life, and there are consequences for both. Today, make an effort to speak words that give life and hope for a new beginning to a coworker, friend, or family member. Pray about your communication—that God will place His words in your mouth so that you proactively handle every negative challenge with grace. It's always our goal for our words to be pleasing to God. Ask God to help you be a blessing and not a hindrance. We never want to be a stumbling block for our brothers and sisters in Christ.

Day 2

STAY OUT OF TROUBLE

Scripture Reading

Watch your tongue and keep your mouth shut, and you will stay out of trouble (Proverbs 21:23 NLT).

Today's Meditation

"If you can't say something nice, don't say anything at all." That's what my mother used to say. Even though you may want to respond, remember you don't always have to. Sometimes the best response is no response. By keeping your mouth shut, you keep your power. But when you open it and the wrong thing comes out, you risk losing your power and your ability to be an effective witness in the body of Christ. We don't always have to share our points of view. Sometimes it's better to keep quiet and avoid starting trouble. Think before you speak today. If your words will cause confusion, don't just blurt them out. Let the Holy Spirit guide you. "God is not the author of confusion, but of peace" (1 Corinthians 14:33).

Day 3

What's on Your Mind?

Scripture Reading

Who can know the Lord's thoughts? Who knows enough to teach him? But we understand these things, for we have the mind of Christ (1 Corinthians 2:16 NLT).

Today's Meditation

As a believer you have access to God's thoughts—through His Son, His Word, and His Spirit. As we spend time with God, our relationship with Him matures. We begin to gain insight and understanding concerning His good plans for our lives. Pray and believe for the mind of Christ. Then allow God's thoughts to lead your actions. What's on your mind matters. If you go throughout the day thinking about nothing but negative things, you're going to self-destruct. Why? Because if you're meditating on negativity, it will only be a matter of time before you start voicing it. Our goal is not to spread negativity, but to spread the Gospel. Keep your mind stayed on the things of God. Cast down negative thoughts and rebellious imaginations. Take them into captivity by faith. Evict the enemy from your mind and move God in.

Day 4

Stand Fast and Believe

Scripture Reading

And whatever you ask in prayer, you will receive, if you have faith (Matthew 21:22 ESV).

Today's Meditation

There will be times when it seems impossible to overcome what you face. With God nothing is impossible. Your faith is the key to overcoming. Don't meditate on doubtful thoughts or speak doubtful words. Doubt turns to unbelief, and it is unbelief that drives a wedge between you and your promised victory. Life's maze of problems can make you feel like there is no chance of ever getting out of the hell that you are experiencing. But God has assured us that "many are the afflictions of the righteous: but the Lord delivereth him out of them all" (Psalm 34:19). There is always hope for the believer.

Day 5

MEDITATE ON THE PROMISES

Scripture Reading

This book of the law shall not depart out of thy mouth; but thou shalt meditate therein day and night, that thou mayest observe to do according to all that is written therein: for then thou shalt make thy way prosperous, and then thou shalt have good success (Joshua 1:8).

Today's Meditation

We are no longer under the law, but covered by grace. However, I believe the principle is that we should not make the mistake of waiting for God to bring us success. He has already blessed us with the greatest success conduit—His Son, Jesus Christ. To receive the success that is promised to us we must first receive Jesus into our lives as Lord and Savior, then by faith believe that we have also received salvation, healing, prosperity, and wholeness. Meditate on the promises in God's Word. Learn them. Believe them. Declare them. Then you will "have good success."

Day 6

OH, WHAT PEACE WE FORFEIT

Scripture Reading

You keep him in perfect peace whose mind is stayed on You, because He trusts in you. Trust in the Lord forever, for the Lord God is an everlasting rock (Isaiah 26:3-4 ESV).

Today's Meditation

As the hymn says, we often forfeit our peace because we fail to take our problems to God. God wants us to cast our cares on Him—not our unbelieving neighbors, disgruntled coworkers, or pessimistic family members. Though everything around you seems to be falling apart, take heart in knowing that God's Word is not. It is solid as an everlasting rock. His word and His love will never fade. He is a part of you, and that part of you is indestructible. It's the part of your life that rebuilds, restores, and resurrects! Nothing is impossible with God.

Day 7

KEEP YOUR HEAD UP

Scripture Reading

Because greater is He that is in you, than he that is in the world (1 John 4:4).

Today's Meditation

The Word and Jesus are one. "In the beginning was the Word, and the Word was with God, and the Word was God" (John 1:1). Jesus lives in you, and He that lives in you is greater and more powerful than any obstacle you face in the world. Don't look down at your problems. Look up at the promise. Your help comes from the Lord, and He is high and lifted up, just as your countenance should be. Keep your head up. Feed your mind, will, imagination, emotions, and intellect with the Word of God. He wants to abide in you. Lift Him up and give Him glory for healing today. By faith call yourself "healthy and prosperous" whether you feel it or not, because in Christ all things, including sickness and disease, are under your feet.

Day 8

Be in Health

Scripture Reading

Beloved, I pray that you may prosper in all things and be in health, just as your soul prospers (3 John 1:2 NKJV)

Today's Meditation

Your soul consists of your mind, will, imagination, emotions, and intellect—all of which God wants to prosper. But God also wants you to prosper in your health. Don't believe the enemy who tells you that you must die of something. God wants you to live a long and prosperous life. Make the choice today to live the life God wants you to have. Let God be true and every man a liar. Don't accept the lies of the enemy. Before you can receive healing, you must first believe that it is God's will for your life. Lift the name of Jesus today and every day.

Day 9

Don't Worry

Scripture Reading

Be anxious for nothing, but in everything by prayer and supplication, with thanksgiving, let your requests be made known to God; and the peace of God, which surpasses all understanding, will guard your hearts and minds through Christ Jesus (Philippians 4:6-7 NKJV).

Today's Meditation

Don't fret—pray. Let God know your concerns about the challenges you face. He cares for you. Thank Him for His love, power, and glory manifesting in your life right now. Thank Him for the peace that is enveloping you and calming you right now, in the name of Jesus. God has not given you a spirit of fear. By faith receive your spirit of power and a sound mind.

The enemy wants you to stress and worry. He wants you to magnify your problem. But Scripture says, "Magnify the Lord" (Psalm 34:3) not "Magnify the problem." Rest in His arms today, knowing that when you pray He hears you, He is mindful of you, and He is your fortress and strong tower. The Lord is your light and salvation; you have nothing to fear.

YOU ARE DELIVERED!

Scripture Reading

He sent His word, and healed them, and delivered them from their destructions (Psalm 107:20).

Today's Meditation

Sometimes we make bad decisions that bring negative consequences in our emotional or physical health—but God offers hope for us. We are able to break free by receiving His forgiveness, not because we've suddenly become perfect, but because of His mercy.

You serve a merciful God who is ready to send His Word to heal you! He sent His Son, Jesus—His only begotten Son—to heal all your diseases. Every emotional sickness, every psychological illness, every physical health challenge must bow down and subject itself to the Word of God. Man's wisdom is finite. He knows only what He has been taught. Medical professionals play a part in the healing process, but God knows all. He has promised to send His Word, heal you, and deliver you from your destructions. Don't be condemned today. Repent; receive His forgiveness. It's free; you don't have to earn it. Jesus already paid for it. Now, lift your hands and offer God a sacrifice of praise for your deliverance!

GOD WILL MAKE HIS WORD COME TRUE

Scripture Reading

Then said the Lord unto me, Thou hast well seen: for I will hasten my word to perform it (Jeremiah 1:12).

Today's Meditation

Looking at your circumstances, you may think there is no way things are going to get better. But don't discount God. He is fully aware of what you are facing and He has heard your cry for help.

Just as He told Jeremiah, He is telling you—His Word will be fulfilled in your life. He cannot lie. The promise of healing is not an empty one. His Word must accomplish what it is sent forth to do. Stay in faith. God's promise to Jeremiah and to us is that no sickness, disease, or trouble that comes against us will overtake or destroy us. If we trust Him and believe His promise, He is faithful to keep His Word. Trust God to show Himself mighty in your time of weakness.

Day 12

RESURRECTION POWER LIVES IN YOU

Scripture Reading

But if the Spirit of Him that raised up Jesus from the dead dwell in you, He that raised up Christ from the dead shall also quicken your mortal bodies by His Spirit that dwelleth in you (Romans 8:11).

Today's Meditation

Today's scripture tells us that the same Spirit who raised Christ from the dead lives inside you and me. We have more power within than we realize. When we accepted Christ as our Lord and Savior, His Spirit came to dwell inside us. That same Spirit raised Christ from the dead and can heal our bodies—if we only believe.

You are delivered from death. You are delivered from disease. You are alive unto God the father, and the same power that raised Christ from the dead is dwelling on the inside of you. Your body is the temple of God. Sickness and disease have no right to overtake your body. Sickness and disease cannot live where Jesus lives!

Day 13

YOU CAN'T WIN WITH PHYSICAL MIGHT

Scripture Reading

For though we walk in the flesh, we do not war according to the flesh. For the weapons of our warfare are not carnal but mighty in God for pulling down strongholds (2 Corinthians 10:3-4 NKJV).

Today's Meditation

You are created in the image of your Father. He is Spirit, and likewise you are a spirit living a human existence. The battle you are facing should be fought using spiritual tools. We fight battles using our faith in the Word. Our human bodies are weak in comparison to our spiritual bodies. The same power that raised Christ from the dead lives in our spirit, and we are mighty and powerful through Him.

God's mighty weapons of faith, hope, love, and prayer are available to us every day to pull down the strongholds of any illness. The Holy Spirit is ready to lead you, comfort you, and encourage you. But we must open our hearts to Him, and we must choose to use the weapons God has given us. It is only when we draw closer to God during our time of weakness that He is able to show himself strong during our toughest time. "Not by might, nor by power, but by My Spirit, saith the Lord" (Zechariah 4:6).

GOD HAS PLANS FOR YOU

Scripture Reading

"For I know the plans I have for you," declares the Lord, "plans to prosper you and not to harm you, plans to give you hope and a future" (Jeremiah 29:11 NIV).

Today's Meditation

This is one of my favorite scriptures. I have it posted on my vision board. I recite it at least three times a day and always offer it to others as a word of encouragement. God has a plan for me and you. His plan is to give us hope and a bright future.

The Lord didn't plan for you to be sick. It is His will that we walk in divine health. He doesn't want us to become so ill that it takes a miracle to cure us. He wants every cell that He created in our bodies to be healthy and strong. If you are experiencing illness, please don't let the enemy tell you that this is what God planned for you. Jeremiah 29:11 reveals God's plan is to prosper you, not make you sick or bedridden. So do not accept sickness and disease as part of your life's plan. Reject it!

Sickness in your body is like an intruder invading your home. Treat illness like you would an intruder—command it to go, in the name of Jesus. Speak to migraines and command them to cease. Speak to cancer and command it to flee from you. You have the authority in Jesus to speak to mountains and command them to be cast into the sea. Don't doubt that it's God's will for you to be healed. Trust in His plan. Wait on Him, and obtain your victory by faith.

YOU ARE INDESTRUCTIBLE

Scripture Reading

We are troubled on every side, yet not distressed; we are perplexed, but not in despair; persecuted, but not forsaken; cast down, but not destroyed (2 Corinthians 4:8-9).

Today's Meditation

Trouble may be coming at you from every direction, but don't give up on the power of Jesus that lives in you. Christ has overcome the world. Use your faith. At our weakest, God is His strongest. So many things happen in life. We never know what to expect from one day to the next. But we do know that God is the same yesterday, today, and forever. His power is the same today, tomorrow, and for eternity. Life isn't always fair, but we can't let the unfair things that happen to us cause us to lose faith in God. We have everlasting life in Christ Jesus, and because we are a part of the Body, we cannot be destroyed. Our Lord is always with us.

Day 16

NOTHING HAS POWER OVER YOU

Scripture Reading

But in that coming day no weapon turned against you will succeed. You will silence every voice raised up to accuse you. These benefits are enjoyed by the servants of the Lord; their vindication will come from Me. I, the Lord, have spoken! (Isaiah 54:17 NLT)

Today's Meditation

The Lord has assured us that no weapon formed against us will succeed in destroying us. That means nothing and no one can come against you and ultimately succeed in a way that will cause you irrevocable damage. Even if you lose your home, job, or, worse still, someone you love, the future still is bright because the Lord your God is an ever-present help in the times of trouble. There have been times in my life when people I thought were on my side turned out to be my biggest enemies. It hurt to know that they weren't really on my side, but were rooting for my failure, and, in some cases, even formulating ways to hurt me. But in every situation God blessed me to rise to the top, even if it seemed that I started out sinking. No man can keep a God-fearing believer down! God will bless you so well that you will shut their mouths. Vengeance is in God's hands. You have the upper hand.

HE'S HERE, THERE, AND EVERYWHERE

Scripture Reading

Behold, I am the Lord, the God of all flesh; is anything too difficult for Me? (Jeremiah 32:27 NASB)

Today's Meditation

The Lord answered Jeremiah's question with a question, "Is anything too difficult for Me?" God is still asking us that today. When I was praying about my son and his drug addiction, God told me, "His ways are not My ways." I didn't understand why He wanted me to do the things He was instructing me to do, but I trusted Him, because He is the Almighty and nothing is too hard for Him—no matter how hard it may seem for me. We must remember that God would not instruct us to do anything that is going to destroy us. Nor will He send us anywhere that He will not be with us. God is everywhere we need Him to be, whenever we need Him. He is what we need, when we need it. Nothing is too hard for Him. Take heart in the fact that your God is the only true God, and He has ultimate authority. He created the heavens and the earth. There is nothing on earth that He is not aware of. What you are facing is no surprise to God. He's already worked it out. You will be victorious.

Day 18

YOU ARE MADE IN HIS IMAGE AND HE IS GREAT

Scripture Reading

Thine, O Lord is the greatness, and the power, and the glory, and the victory, and the majesty: for all that is in the heaven and in the earth is Thine; Thine is the Kingdom, O Lord, and Thou art exalted as head above all (1 Chronicles 29:11).

Today's Meditation

Don't let your atmosphere determine how you feel about yourself or what your attitude will be. Circumstances change, and if you allow outside influences to dictate your attitude it will be changing like the weather. Some days you will be angry; other days you may be sad, and only on a few occasions when everything goes your way will you be glad. But how often does *everything* go your way?

To have a winning attitude you must know who your God is. King David knew how awesome and wonderful his God was and he showed that in his prayer of praise. It's not enough just to know how wonderful God is; you also have to remember that you are created in His image. So if He is wonderful, so are you!

The Scripture says everything in Heaven and earth is the Lord's. Your God owns it all. There is nothing in heaven or on earth that God does not rule over. You serve a mighty God who wants you to walk in victory. Every resource that you need, He is able to supply because He owns it all.

HE HAS YOUR BACK

Scripture Reading

Contend, O Lord, with those who contend with me; fight against those who fight against me (Psalm 35:1 ESV)!

Today's Meditation

David prayed to God for justice. He was angry, hurt, and confused. Why were people trying to kill him? What had he done to deserve such horrible treatment? Oftentimes we find ourselves in situations where we don't understand why people are treating us the way that they are. Their actions are unfair, and, in some cases, unjust. God does not want us to feel that we have to accept cruelty from anyone. He promises that He will protect us and deliver us from every affliction (see Psalm 34:19). Cruel people cannot break you unless you allow them to. If you don't change the way you respond to their behavior, you will stress yourself out and possibly even end up sick. Do what a winner would do. Change your perception. See the cruel behavior as a challenge, an opportunity. The opportunity to be blessed for doing something that pleases God—loving your enemy.

Ain't No Mountain High Enough

Scripture Reading

Who shall separate us from the love of Christ? shall tribulation, or distress, or persecution, or famine, or nakedness, or peril, or sword (Romans 8:35)?

Today's Meditation

Nothing you're facing can ever separate you from the love of God. It doesn't matter if it's a struggle in your daily life, relationship, on your job, or related to your health. No matter what in our lives is making us bend and causing us to feel like we're about to break, it's nothing that can keep God from coming to our rescue. Just because we go through difficult times that doesn't mean we are unloved. Romans 8:34 assures us that Jesus is interceding for us in heaven. Our sins have been removed because of Jesus. Don't let the situation you face make you believe that you have gotten so far away that God's love cannot reach you. He has not abandoned you, and He never will—Christ never will.

WINGS LIKE AN EAGLE

Scripture Reading

But they that wait upon the Lord shall renew their strength; they shall mount up with wings as eagles; they shall run, and not be weary; and they shall walk, and not faint (Isaiah 40:31).

Today's Meditation

Before you can hope to live a victorious life, you must first believe God loves you no matter what and He wants what is best for you in every situation. When you believe that, you will find strength that you didn't know you had. Right now you may be feeling weak and unsure of yourself. That's because you've forgotten that you serve a God who loves you, not because you are perfect, but because His Son Jesus Christ has reconciled your relationship with Him. You see, it is not through your righteousness that you're entitled to victory and blessings; it's through the righteousness of our Lord and Savior, Jesus Christ. He bore your sins. You don't have to. Stop beating yourself up and trying to atone for your own sins. Christ has already done that. All you have to do is accept, receive, and believe. There is no sin that you've committed that Christ didn't know about the day He laid down His life on the cross for you. You are forgiven. Because you are for-given, you are entitled to all that heaven has to offer in Jesus Christ. Knowing that and reminding yourself of it regularly will give you renewed strength.

Day 22

YOU CAN BE AFRAID AND STILL BE COURAGEOUS

Scripture Reading

Wait on the Lord: be of good courage, and He shall strengthen thine heart: wait, I say, on the Lord (Psalm 27:14).

Today's Meditation

Courage is not the absence of fear. Some fear speaking in public, while others fear flying, or insects. I've been told that I do very well at public speaking. However, I have to admit that it scares me. I always imagine myself making a mistake and everyone pointing and laughing. There are so many things in life that we can be afraid of. The important thing though is not to allow fear to stop you from moving forward. The Scripture says to be of "good courage." I know when I was praying for my son during the period that he was battling drug addiction, there was a time when I started to become afraid. God wasn't moving fast enough for me, and it seemed my son would surely be lost forever or, worse, I'd be planning his funeral. But God wants us to be courageous. Courage will allow us to remain in faith. When He sees that we are brave in Him, then He will strengthen our hearts. Just because we are trembling in fear doesn't mean we can't still be trusting in faith! Faith pleases God.

FLAWED BUT FAITHFUL

Scripture Reading

Hope in the Lord and keep His way. He will exalt you to inherit the land; when the wicked are destroyed, you will see it (Psalm 37:34 NIV).

Today's Meditation

The entire 37th Psalm is a motivational read for anyone looking for inspiration. David reminds us that God is always with the righteous, ready to protect and provide. Instead of hoping in our careers and people, our hope must be in the Lord. *To hope* means to have confidence that the outcome of your situation will be a positive one. As believers, this is the hope that we have because of our Lord and Savior's self-sacrifice. Our Father in Heaven desires to exalt us and give us victory.

We need only please God with the desires of our hearts, and He will honor our efforts. He will protect us and keep us. We don't have to worry about how we're going to make it; we just have to have faith that God will exalt us because of our faithfulness and our right standing through Jesus Christ, not our religious works or flawless personalities.

Day 24

You Are a Winner!

Scripture Reading

Watch ye, stand fast in the faith, quit you like men, be strong. Let all your things be done with charity (1 Corinthians 16:13-14).

Today's Meditation

Paul loved the Corinthians. He wanted them to succeed. In his letter to them, he encouraged them to remember the Gospel that they had been taught and stand fast on its promises. Life can be hard, especially when problems come from many directions at once. You may be facing one of the most difficult days of your life, but you have hope in the grace of God. Like Paul instructed the Church at Corinth to do, you must remember the power of the Gospel and stand fast in it. *Stand fast* is another way of saying stay firm. Don't waver in the midst of today's conflict. Don't let the situation make you think that you're going to lose.

You are a winner in Christ. No matter what the outcome today, ultimately God has promised you will not be destroyed. Every tongue that rises against you, you shall condemn (see Isaiah 54:17). The day will come that the truth will come out. You will be vindicated.

YOU HAVE SUPERNATURAL STRENGTH

Scripture Reading

Then he answered and spake unto me, saying, This is the word of the Lord unto Zerubbabel, saying, Not by might, nor by power, but by my spirit, saith the Lord of hosts (Zechariah 4:6).

Today's Meditation

Too often we focus on our own strength, and that makes us hesitant to take risks or push ourselves beyond our physical, financial, or educational limitations. There is a heavenly Kingdom where all things are perfect and every great power exists. It is from that spiritual world that our greatest strength and ability comes. Why rely only on human strength when supernatural strength is available by His Spirit?

Don't limit yourself only to what you can do. It is vain for us to worry about how things will get done because we are focusing only on our own human ability. In Scripture, Zerubbabel was tasked with rebuilding the temple and was concerned because the responsibility was so great in the face of adversity. God told Zerubbabel that neither might nor power would help him to accomplish his goal and overcome the adversity, but rather the Spirit of God. How much can you accomplish through the power of the Spirit who knows all, sees all, and knew you before you were even formed in your mother's womb (see Jeremiah 1:5)? Even if there is a daunting task before you, don't limit yourself, but most importantly don't limit the possibilities of what the Spirit can accomplish through a willing heart.

What You Do for Him Matters

Scripture Reading

Therefore, my beloved brethren, be ye stedfast, unmoveable, always abounding in the work of the Lord, forasmuch as ye know that your labour is not in vain in the Lord (1 Corinthians 15:58).

Today's Meditation

In my experience, more often than not, the Lord takes His time. It's during this time that our faith develops, and we learn the power of perseverance. James 1:3 tells us that the testing of our faith produces patience. This is how we receive the promises, through faith and patience (see Hebrews 6:12). The worst thing we can do is become discouraged because things aren't happening fast enough.

Years ago, I had a good friend who worked in the ministry. She was very diligent in attending services, studying her lessons, and developing programs for various auxiliaries. But when the time came for praise to be given, she was always looked over. She didn't understand why her hard work wasn't being acknowledged. She talked to me about giving up. Her thought was that because no one recognized her work, why should she do it? I told my friend what I am telling you today.

Her time spent teaching, planning, and coordinating was not in vain. Even though being overlooked was a hard pill to swallow, she shouldn't allow herself to become discouraged. Man did not give her the talent to do what she had accomplished; they had simply reaped the benefits. The same is true for us. We must do our good works to glorify the Father. When we work enthusiastically for the glory of God, He is pleased and our reward comes from Him.

Day 27

BE ENCOURAGED

Scripture Reading

For it is written, He shall give His angels charge over thee, to keep thee (Luke 4:10).

Today's Meditation

This is one of the most inspirational Bible verses in the book of Luke. It shows God's love in the form of protection. I've prayed it over my sons on more than one occasion. Especially for my oldest, while we were standing in faith for his deliverance from addiction, and still today in prayer. But what I find most fascinating about this Scripture is who is quoting it—satan. Not one of the disciples, not Jesus, not a lay person, but the devil himself during his attempt to talk Jesus into jumping off the highest point of the temple (see Luke 4:9). The enemy wanted to stop Jesus from succeeding in His mission to redeem the world, so he tried to manipulate Him through temptations.

Be encouraged. Though temptation to quit comes against you, you have already been equipped to overcome the temptation. James 4:7 says, "Resist the devil, and he will flee from you." An even greater comfort comes from believing First Corinthians 10:13: "There hath no temptation taken hold of you but such as is common to man: but God is faithful, who will not suffer you to be tempted above that ye are able; but will with the temptation also make a way to escape, that ye may be able to bear it." The devil is a liar. If God has placed a mission in your heart, then He will accomplish that good work in you (see Psalm 138:8).

PLANT YOUR VICTORY BANNER AHEAD OF TIME

Scripture Reading

Be strong and of a good courage; be not afraid, neither be thou dismayed: for the Lord thy God is with thee whithersoever thou goest (Joshua 1:9).

Today's Meditation

God commanded Joshua three times to be strong and have good courage and assured him of His constant presence if His commandments were obeyed (see Joshua 1:8-9). He promised, "The eternal God is thy refuge, and underneath are the everlasting arms: and He shall thrust out the enemy from before thee; and shall say, Destroy them" (Deuteronomy 33:27).

Knowing the Lord and obeying His commandments are the two main ingredients for the God kind of courage. *Courage* is greatness of heart, a spirit to meet danger, and boldness. El Shaddai, the All-Sufficient and Mighty One is on your side. He is Jehovah Nissi, the Lord your Victory Banner (see Exodus 17:15). Think about that for a moment. Normally a victory flag would be flown after a battle, but because God is our Banner of victory, we can fly our victory flag as soon as a faith fight begins. Because of their obedience, Moses and Joshua were assured of God's presence in their time of need. Today we have the blessed assurance of the greater One who lives in us. First John 4:4 says, "Greater is He that is in you, than he that is in the world." We have to take our eyes off what is happening in front of us and focus on the greater spiritual battle that is taking place. With the whole armor of God, we can and will be victorious!

BLESSED TO BE A BLESSING

Scripture Reading

Not rendering evil for evil, or railing for railing: but contrariwise blessing; knowing that ye are thereunto called, that ye should inherit a blessing (1 Peter 3:9).

Today's Meditation

We, as Christians, are consecrated, set apart, and highly favored. When God blesses us, it is more than houses, cars, and expensive jewelry. God's blessings are designed to make you stand out. You are peculiar, and what makes you peculiar is that you are chosen to be a royal, holy priest for Him. In this role you are to be a blessing, not only to those around you, but first and foremost to Him who has called you out of darkness into His glorious light. You are consecrated, highly favored, a holy priest. You are awesome!

When you obey the voice of God and keep His commandments (see Exodus 16:5-6), you will hear His voice and be able to lead your life in a manner that pleases Him and opens the doors for abundant blessings to flow in your life, and through you to others around you. You see, you being positive, blessed, and highly favored isn't just about you; it's about helping to improve the outlook of others with whom you come in contact. When you put yourself in a position to be blessed and to be a blessing, God's blessing will come upon you and overtake you. Are you ready for blessings? Are you ready to abound in every area of your life, to have victory over your enemies, and to live peacefully and in good health? Of course you are!

Day 30

YOUR LIFE MAY BE A MESS...BUT GRACE!

Scripture Reading

Let us then approach God's throne of grace with confidence, so that we may receive mercy and find grace to help us in our time of need (Hebrews 4:16 NIV).

Today's Meditation

Though God has this bright future planned for you, there are things you need to do to ensure that you reach your place of destiny in life. The enemy wants to keep you from your destiny by keeping you focused on the mistakes of your past, but *grace* has you covered. Don't waste another day over-thinking your "shortcomings," "flaws," and "sins." Instead, meditate on the Word and keep your heart and mind filled with the inspiration of the Holy Spirit. Study day and night so that you will know what God's Word has to say about your present and your future.

God promises if you do this, you will make your way prosperous and you will have good success (see Joshua 1:8). Let the Holy Spirit be your guide in all that you do. Ask for guidance so that you know that the path you are taking to reach your destiny is ordained by God. Keep the words of your mouth in line with the Word of God's Gospel. It will transform your life. Romans 1:16 says the Gospel is the power of God. Don't be ashamed to declare it over your life daily.

Always have an attitude of gratitude and grace. Extend forgiveness to others and know in your heart that God is extending that same grace and forgiveness to you. You are fearfully and wonderfully made in God's image (see Psalm 139:14).

SHOUT WITH A VOICE OF TRIUMPH

Scripture Reading

And all this assembly shall know that the Lord saveth not with sword and spear: for the battle is the Lord's, and He will give you into our hands (1 Samuel 17:47).

Today's Meditation

When David faced Goliath he shouted: "Thou comest to me with a sword, and with a spear, and with a shield: but I come to thee in the name of the Lord of hosts, the God of the armies of Israel" (1 Samuel 17:45). Your problems and challenges are no match for the Lord of Hosts. You must believe with all your heart, and never doubt, that God would deliver you, just like David believed that his God would deliver him from Goliath. No matter how big the giant or how many people are telling you that the giant is too big to conquer, stand and declare victory.

Use the Word (Scripture) that God has placed in your heart and speak victory, put on your spiritual armor, plant your victory banner, and continue to pray without ceasing. As you claim your victory daily, refuse to allow people and circumstances around you to cause you to lose faith. When doubt tries to come and steal your faith, arrest it with the Word of God. Declare that you and your house will serve the Lord.

ABOUT LYNN R. DAVIS

The mother of two boys, Lynn R. Davis lives on the outskirts of Austin, Texas. She is the oldest of six siblings and the doting aunt of five nieces and eleven nephews. Her main goal in life is to encourage, inspire, and uplift. She holds a bachelor's degree in business administration from Huston-Tillotson University at Austin and a Master of Science in leadership and ethics from St. Edward's University at Austin.

For more information about the author, please visit LynnRDavis.com or email lynnrdavis@hotmail.com.